THE SLUMS OF
LEICESTER

A Photographic Record Illustrated by Contemporary Accounts

2009

Edited by Ned Newitt

Acknowledgements

Thanks are due to: Shirley Aucott, Peter Bunney, Nigel Daykin, Philip French, Colin Hyde, Jonathan Parkes-Bowen, Peter Soulsby MP, George Wilson, the editor of *Leicester Mercury* and the staff at the Records Office for Leicester, Leicestershire and Rutland. Finally, to Malcolm Elliott, whose pioneering work *Victorian Leicester* (1979) laid the basis for much in this book.

Photographic Acknowledgements

Except where stated the photographs and maps found in this book are from the collection of the Record Office for Leicester, Leicestershire and Rutland. In some cases prints of the same photograph are in more than one collection.

Cover photograph: A detail of Eaton Square (Upper) Brown Street (see page 131)

Back cover: The narrow passage at the rear of Court A, Highcross Street (see page 97)

About the Author

Ned Newitt was born in Southend-on-Sea in 1946. He studied at Cardiff College of Art and came to Leicester in 1971. For many years, he was an art teacher at Wreake Valley College.

From 1984–2003 he was a Leicester City Councillor, holding various prominent positions, including chair of the Housing Committee, a position in which he was responsible for both Council housing and housing renewal. He was made an honorary Alderman in 2007.

In 1983 he initiated the Leicester Oral History Archive and has subsequently researched the development of Council housing in Leicester.

He has published *The Anthology of Leicester Chartist Song, Poetry and Verse* (2006) and *A People's History of Leicester* (2008). Aside from history and politics, he is a keen amateur jazz saxophone player and runs the record label Mellotone Records, which specialises in historic hot dance band recordings. He lives in Leicester.

This paperback edition published in Great Britain in 2013 by DB Publishing, an imprint of JMD Media Ltd

ISBN 978-185983-933-1

Printed and bound in Great Britain by Marston Book Services Ltd, Oxfordshire

Contents

Victor Cottages were approached through a narrow entry from Victor Street (previously Victoria Street), which was situated off Lee Street. This yard was common to Nos 1–3 Victor Street and Nos 1–4 Victor Cottages, which were back-to-back with a factory situated on the left. The lean-to building was the wash house for the front houses and the door on the right was the back entrance to No. 1½ Victor Street. The common tap in the yard was fixed against the corner of the wash house and there were three WCs for the use of the seven tenants, with another common wash house for the use of the court houses. In 1926, following the landlord's refusal to repair the cottages, the Council stepped in to do the work. At the time of this picture, c.1938, the cottages were awaiting demolition.

The Slums of Leicester: An Introduction

For the last 150 years, Leicester's motto of *Semper Eadem* (Always the Same) has been a polite fiction. During the 19th century, the rapid urban expansion of housing and factories transformed what had been a market town into an industrial city. In the 20th century slum clearance changed the face of Leicester again. Vast swathes of housing, close to the centre of town, were demolished and new roads, Council housing and industrial estates took their place. Between 1932 and 1976 around 16,000 houses were 'cleared'. Until then, the slums had been home to thousands of people who had to live in conditions that were frequently cramped and unhealthy. This book is intended to give a picture of these poorer districts of Leicester from surviving photographs, maps and contemporary accounts.

There is no scientific definition of a slum and the accepted view of what constituted one has changed over time. The Council's view of what is unfit housing has also changed radically. Up until 1939, Leicester's poorest housing was situated close to the centre of town. It covered an area stretching from today's Dysart Way round to the Holiday Inn, bounded by the river and canal on one side and the line of Humberstone Road and the High Street on the other. There were also small pockets of slums around Wellington Street, Brown Street (the Phoenix Theatre area) and Great Holme Street. These were not the respectable Victorian terraces which are still around today, but older, smaller houses mostly built before the introduction of the local building bye-laws. After 1945, the largest concentration of unfit housing in the city was located in the area to the east of Wharf Street, and it is for this reason that the area is now remembered as the epicentre of Leicester's slum districts. Before the war there had been other areas of the city which the Council considered to be far worse than Wharf Street, but because these areas were demolished pre-1939 the existence of these older districts faded has from the collective memory. By the 1960s and 1970s, slum clearance reached into Highfields, Belgrave and the West End. There were even small clearance areas in Knighton, Aylestone, Humberstone and Evington.

In 1831, Leicester had a population of 38,904 and by 1901 it had grown to 211,579, spurred by the demand for labour from the town's expanding hosiery and boot and shoe trades. This growing workforce was accommodated in cheap, badly built cottages centred around a courtyard only accessible through narrow entries. As the town grew, tall factories and warehouses often encroached, casting an all-pervading gloom on the nearby cottages. These densely packed courtyards all too often lacked sunlight, fresh air and proper ventilation. The need to be able to walk to work meant that housing had to be close to the factories, and for those living on low incomes, affected by fluctuations in trade, the low rents of these cottages were crucial. With landlords only interested in the rent that their agents collected, these cheaply built cottages were continually getting out of repair.

Many of Leicester's landlords seem to have had a social background not that far removed from their tenants. These were not factory owners, but small capitalists who bought houses as an investment sometimes with a view to providing an income for their old age. Many, like Bailey, Bateman and Cramant, gave their names to the yards or courts which were often land developments at the rear or close by to where they lived. Thomas Bland, who developed and owned many slums, started out as a bricklayer and lived on Redcross Street in the heart of a slum district.

Most of these cottages had just two rooms – one up and one down. Cooking would have taken place over a fire or on a range, there would have been no internal water supply and washing would have been done outside. Many were effectively back-to-back houses as they had no rear doors or windows.[1] They were frequently built with inadequate foundations and

---

1. These were sometimes called rear wall blank or dwellings with a single aspect.

People sitting outside No. 26 Lower Grove Street for air during hot weather, probably in the summer of 1937. This view was taken from Grovesnor Street looking towards the back of Gower Street houses. Some of the front houses sat back-to-back with houses in the rear yards. No. 26 was the house situated next to the entry on the right. The tenants were rehoused on Gallards Hill and Braybrook Road in November 1937 and the houses demolished in February 1938. (Author)

thin brickwork. Floors were usually lain directly on the earth and the cottages lacked proper drains. Often, the shoddiness of the original construction, coupled with the lack of repairs, the frequent change of tenants and the ravages of the tenants themselves, brought about the complete ruin of the cottages.

In the 1840s, death and disease were shown to be more prevalent in streets with no drainage. Water supplies and drainage were inadequate, especially in the newer working-class districts. Until 1853, Leicester had no supply of piped water. Water was drawn either from wells or from cisterns which collected rainwater from the roofs of houses. Much of the water from the wells was contaminated by seepage from cesspits or from holes from privies which had been dug right down to the water seam.

Apart from the housing built in the area of what was the old walled town, which was on slightly higher ground, virtually all the new working-class housing was built on low-lying land which provided little natural fall for sewers and was frequently exposed to flooding. Sometimes houses could be flooded to a depth of two or three feet with water. Floods would bring up the sewage and leave behind a deposit of insanitary mud. The beneficial side effect of this topography was that it was impossible to construct cellar dwellings in the town.

In the first half of the 19th century, landlords and developers had a free hand. Laissez-faire was the order of the day and it was assumed that market forces would meet need and dictate standards. Despite the reforming credentials of the Liberal Council, which held

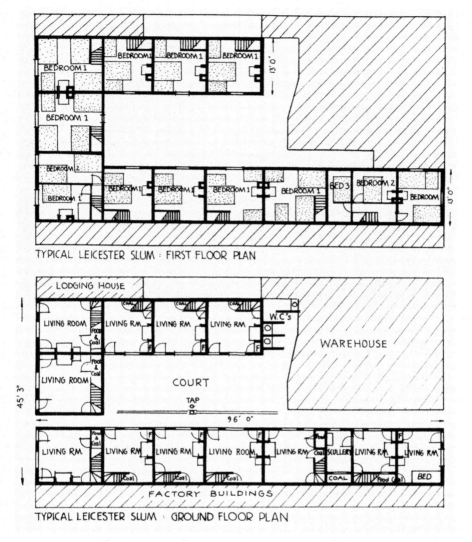

TYPICAL LEICESTER SLUM : FIRST FLOOR PLAN

TYPICAL LEICESTER SLUM : GROUND FLOOR PLAN

From a drawing by J.S. Fyfe, A.R.I.B.A, the city housing architect, 1935.

power from 1835 onwards, little was done to regulate the construction of housing. From 1839, the Corporation had disposed of land for working-class housing with little stipulation about building standards. However, the Corporation's appointment of the veteran ex-Jacobin and Chartist George Bown as Inspector of Nuisances signalled the beginnings of change. His report on the sanitary state of the town also recommended the payment of medical men to certify the existence of such nuisances. In October 1846, doctors Buck and Barclay thus became the first medical officers appointed by a local Council in Britain. In their first report they stressed the importance of a proper system of drainage, the problem of polluted water and the nuisance caused by pig keeping. They proposed five bye-laws: pig keeping within 30 to 40ft of a dwelling was to be prohibited;

Nos 1–6 Cramant's Yard at the rear of No. 54 King Street, c.1984. These are the only courtyard slums in Leicester to have survived to the present day. In 1841, No. 54 King Street was occupied by Hannah Cramant and her family, and altogether 22 people lived in these six cottages. They were built c.1820 and featured horizontal sliding 'Yorkshire' sash windows. The difficulty of producing large sheets of glass meant that small-paned windows were common before 1850. The upper rooms were floored with lime concrete on rushes and the unusual small brick-arched openings on the ground floor were either for ventilating the larders or for deliveries. Although they were scheduled for demolition in 1958 the Council did not compulsorily purchase them and they were left unoccupied for many years. In 1984, they became listed buildings and were refurbished. An atrium was added and the cottages were then incorporated into the Weavers pub. In 2008, they became home to the Cottage Nursery. (Author)

cesspools and privy holes were to be emptied on a regular basis; the keeping of night soil in yards was also to be prohibited; stench traps were to be fitted on drains; and new streets were to have proper drains. John Buck also urged that a regulation be introduced which would prohibit the building of houses back-to-back or without means of through ventilation. From the early 1850s the Corporation began to disallow such plans. Unfortunately, this was not retrospective and many of the worst courts and cottages had already been built in this manner.

The Council's Inspector of Nuisances dealt with the problems caused by leaking and overflowing cesspools, foul and offensive drains and accumulations of dung, as well as nuisances like 'tripe boiling'. He could order the cleansing and limewashing of filthy houses and could seek the closure of unfit dwellings.

In 1854 closing orders were served on the houses in Porkshop Yard. This was the nickname given to Hextall's Yard on Mansfield Street owned by Mrs Abigail Hextall, who also lived in the yard. The 18 houses on the site were described by the Inspector of Nuisances as being occupied as usual by the 'lowest class of persons and are in a very filthy and unwholesome condition'. In 1849, William Ranger had described these houses as

Round chimney stacks were a common feature of working-class housing built prior to the 1859 bye-laws. Prior to its demolition in the 1960s, this chimney stack was on a house in East Street. No such round chimney stacks seem to have survived in central Leicester. (Newarke Houses Museum)

being 'of one room each, at first used as pigstyes, but the speculation failing, they were converted into dwellings each 14ft by 10ft and 6ft 6ins high with an average of five persons in each room. At one end of this yard there is a large house let in separate apartments which, like the common lodging houses, is a nest of fever and disease. The relieving officer makes use of these lodging houses for lodging casual paupers'. Despite its powers, the Council did not demolish these houses but instead, following improvements, allowed them to be relet.

In 1859, Leicester's first local building bye-laws were introduced. They halted the building of back-to-back houses by requiring the provision of a back access.[2] A minimum ceiling height of 8ft 6in downstairs and 8ft upstairs was specified along with minimum space standards at the side or rear of houses. After 1868, the Council gained the power to close any property thought to be unfit, without first having to go through the courts. In 1881, all exterior walls were required to be nine inches thick, and in 1908 the minimum yard size was increased from 150sq ft to 250sq ft.

Leicester's early activity in public health may well have been a response by the Council leaders to address working-class issues. In the early 1850s, radicals like John Biggs had made common cause with the ex-Chartists, and their former long-standing leader John Markham was now a Councillor and a member of the Highways and Sewerage Committee. The new bye-laws encouraged the construction of wider connected streets, rather than enclosed courts. Unfortunately, too many of these streets were long, treeless and monotonous. Bye-law housing was especially appropriate for the development of new areas where the rectilinear layout of streets and terraces could be imposed over open land. In Leicester, this can be seen best in Highfields, Belgrave and the West End. Though the bye-laws signalled a distinct advance in building standards, they were not onerous and therefore did not stop cottages being built in confined spaces at the rear of other houses. These cottages were allowed, however, provided there was a living room and kitchen downstairs.

It was in the poor districts of pre-bye-law housing that infant mortality was highest and incomes and rents were lowest. Joseph Dare's reports, written annually from 1844 to 1877, repeatedly drew attention to the evils of houses without back doors or proper ventilation and

---

2. While back-to-back houses were still being built in Leeds in the 1930s, the last court house was built in Leicester in 1892.

Slum dwellers in the Abbey Street area, c.1930. (Author)

he described some of the appalling conditions found in these crowded districts. In 1851, John Buck reported on the summer epidemic of diarrhoea which killed many of the elderly and very young. By 1871 this yearly scourge was killing one in four Leicester children before their first birthday. As a result, Leicester had a child mortality rate which was twice the national average and on a par with London, Manchester and Liverpool. This sad state of affairs continued right into the early 20th century. The slum area on low ground, bounded on one side by the Willow Brook, canal and river and the stretch of Humberstone Road to High Street on the air, was consequently known as the 'diarrhoea area'. The cause of this annual epidemic was hotly debated. Summer heat, gas from the sewers and the lack of 'mothercraft' on the part of women working in factories were all blamed. However, the real reason was the town's inadequate sewers and the resultant insanitary conditions.

Originally, many houses were built with midden privies and ashpits. As the town grew it proved difficult to replace them with flush toilets since the sewers could not cope with the extra volume of water. In the 1870s an interim solution of pail closets was introduced in the poorer districts. These were galvanised buckets containing some disinfectant which were emptied by the 'night soil' men and carted away.

In 1898, a new sewage system powered by the new Abbey pumping station enabled the Town Council to phase out the use of pail closets in the slums. Ashpits were removed as pail closets were converted into water closets. By 1904, 5,397 pail closets were replaced and the programme was virtually complete, except for a few isolated cases. (At that time there were about 40,000 inhabited houses in the town.) Leicester's public health improved dramatically, overtaking Nottingham and many other large towns where the majority of people still used pail closets, privies and middens. Although the disparity in health between the rich and poor areas of Leicester remained marked, this early intervention by the Council distinguished it as a 'progressive' authority.

At the turn of the century the level of overcrowding in Leicester was less than in many

A woman filling a tin bath from a well-lagged common tap, c.1954. Although this photograph is not labelled, it is likely that it was taken in the Wharf Street area. (Newarke Houses Museum)

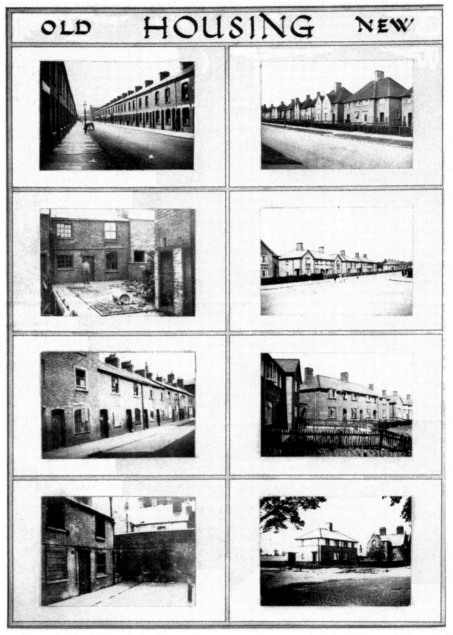

This contrast of new Council housing with the slums made by the City Council's housing architects dates from the mid-1930s. Unfortunately, the whereabouts of the slums were not identified. (Author)

other cities and there was considerable debate as to the extent of Leicester's 'slum problem'. Despite the town's newly acquired progressive reputation, the issue of poor housing became a constant theme for the new Independent Labour Party and a cornerstone of local Labour policy for the decades to come.

In the early 20th century it was usual for houses in the poorer districts to share outside flush toilets and water supplies. Some cottages had neither a scullery to put a copper in or even a communal wash house outside. Where these existed, a copper heated by a coal or wood fire would supply the hot water for the weekly wash of several families. In some cases, washing was made more inconvenient by the lack of waste pipes on sinks. In 1924, 80 per cent of the houses in Wyggeston and Newton Wards had to share toilets. In about a third of cases there were more than two houses to one toilet. According to the Medical Officer of Health: 'apart from the inconvenience and one which cuts across modern ideas of decency and refinement, it is a menace to health'.

Prior to World War One, some demolition of the 'worst' houses had taken place, though this was generally on a piecemeal basis. Although it was claimed that some 2,137 dwellings had been demolished between 1892 and 1914, in fact only 197 houses had been condemned as unfit. While the Council's health inspectors were very active in the regulation of 'nuisances', their remit did not extend to large-scale clearance. It is likely that most of these demolitions were undertaken to enable road-widening schemes, the building of factories and the construction of the Great Central Railway.

Following World War One, the dire shortage of housing in Leicester meant that the Council did not resume its very limited attempts to close and demolish some of the worst local slums until the mid-1920s. Instead, its strategy was to seek the improvement of slums. When landlords increased the rent, the Health Department was able to step in using the 1919 Housing Act to ensure that a property was in reasonable repair before allowing the rent increase. Where there were several houses sharing a common yard and lavatories, a landlord would be required to provide extra toilets or an internal water supply. This was achieved by means of inspections and by serving landlords with notices to abate nuisances. However, often the prospect of increased rents was still not enough to persuade owners to do the necessary work.

Although the Council was now building houses for the working classes, only the better-off workers could afford the rent. It had been hoped that as new Council houses were built the worst housed would somehow filter up into the better accommodation vacated by those who had moved to the new estates. Despite the building of the Saffron and South Braunstone and Coleman Road estates, there was still a shortage of housing and the slums were not emptying. Many of the slums, described by Tom Barclay in the 1890s, had been slums for many years and they were still so in the mid-1930s and even the early 1950s. In 1932, at a time when low interest rates and a drop in the price of materials would have enabled Councils to deliver more houses to those on low incomes, the government took the view that private enterprise was now so large that local Councils should no longer build for general need. Local authorities were told to restrict themselves to slum clearance and rehousing.

The first major slum clearance scheme was for 235 houses in the Green Street-Sandacre Street area and was approved by the City Council in 1929; however, the scheme was delayed until the Council gained new legal powers under the 1930 Greenwood Housing Act. Following a public inquiry and the arrangement of terms with the owners, the ministry gave its final consent to clearance in February 1932. In April the first families moved out to their new houses on Tailby Road.

Although there was an outward political consensus about the need to do something about the slums, there was disagreement about what that meant in practice and these

*Above: a view taken from the back
window of a house on Colton
Street. It shows cottages adjacent
to St George's churchyard, near
the* Leicester Mercury *building.
This photograph was taken on 15
October 1908.*

*Right: The more substantial
houses built to replace those
shown below. These were
demolished in the 1960s.*

*Right: Nos 10–12 Colton
Street, next to the King
Buildings, in 1908. They were
presumably demolished shortly
after.*

Above: Nos 20–26 Thames Street in the 1930s. In the 1850s this street was often flooded with 'offensive sewage'. In the 1930s, these houses were improved and the photograph above left shows newly built sculleries and outside toilets with flat roofs. The newly erected fences created individual gardens for each property, replacing a common yard and shared toilets. (Author)

differences arose during the discussions over the long-term strategy for slum clearance. The Medical Officer of Health Killick Millard believed that there were no real 'plague spots' to be swept away at any cost and that where there were areas not bad enough to be dealt with as clearance areas these could be dealt with through a combination of selective demolition and the repair of old houses. This was not the view of all the Council's officers, but it presented itself as something of a lifeline to the landlords' lobby. While the new Housing Act did provide the opportunity for houses to be improved rather than demolished, many felt that it also offered opportunities for landlords to drag the whole process through the courts and delay any action at all. Clearance was regarded as the swifter and neater solution to a problem that had seemed intractable. The policy of clearance rather than selective demolition was the proposal of the Liberal chairman of the Health Committee, Teddy Hincks, and was supported by the Labour Group.

Outside of the clearance areas, the Health Department aimed to convert houses with common yards and common sanitary conveniences to houses with separate yards, WCs, internal sinks and taps. Though a substantial number of houses were given additional amenities, its scale of work was small in comparison to the size of the problem and many houses still had shared toilets, common yards and external water supplies into the 1950s.

The second slum clearance area in the Redcross Street and Thornton Lane area was fiercely opposed by the Conservatives and some Liberals, who believed that most of the old properties could be improved. At that time the Property Owners' Association included leading Conservative Councillors, as well as the chairman of the Housing Committee. However, by the late 1930s opposition to slum clearance had crumbled. Killick Millard had retired as Medical Officer of Health and his place taken by Dr MacDonald, who oversaw the pre-war and most of the post-war clearances in the 1950s.

During the 1930s tenants were moved en bloc from the old, crowded neighbourhoods. Records show that neighbours were frequently moved to adjacent houses in the same road. Although this must have had the effect of preserving local communities, it was more the result of administrative convenience rather than any deliberate plan. In fact, the records also show that tenants from different areas like Park Street, off Wellington Street, and

In between 18 and 20 Grundon Street was the entry to Abbey Cottages, built in 1876. Three doors close together were a common sight in the older areas of Leicester. The middle door was generally a passageway through to another block of houses built off the road on back lands. This photograph is dated 1963.

Dyers Yard, off Belgrave Gate, all ended up in houses on Hand Avenue, North Braunstone. Apart from George Street, there were no inner-city sites being developed for rehousing. Tenants from 78 different clearance areas scattered around the city were concentrated in North Braunstone and Northfields estates. This situation was dictated by the financial regime set out for rehousing by the government and so the City Council was unable to offer tenants much choice. Specific clearance areas were allocated to new estates and tenants did not appear to have a say in where they went. Even before the first house had been built, the *Braunstone Tenants Gazette* had published a plea that the new rehousing area planned for the north of the estate should not be stigmatised with the word 'slum'. This was not to be the case. Not only were North and South Braunstone physically separated from each other by a park, but they were also divided socially as well. Higher rents for the larger Council houses on the early parts of the estate ensured that only the more respectable sections of the working class were represented. The end of general needs building meant that only families from the slums were moved to North Braunstone.

When they had lived in the centre of town, poorer families had benefitted from their informal local connections which had enabled them to live on very little money. Family networks, casual work, second-hand shops, pawnbrokers, credit in shops and the proximity of the market place all provided a cushion against poverty. But the black economy which sustained so many families in the centre of town was not to be found on the outskirts. With so many displaced, uprooted and poor families from crowded slum streets struggling to settle in a new location, the need for social support was paramount, yet this was neither foreseen nor provided for.

As the old neighbourhoods were reduced to rubble, the difficulties caused by concentrating so many poor and needy families into the Northfields and North Braunstone estates soon became apparent. The allocation of whole clearance areas to specific estates had everything to do with expediting the programme of demolition and rehousing: little thought was given either to preserving communities or preventing the development of ghettos. It was probably hoped that the physical improvement in housing conditions was sufficient to counter poverty and disadvantage.

Slum clearance offered the Corporation the opportunity to replan some of Leicester's central areas. Already some roads in the Bedford Street area had been replanned to enable plots of land off Belgrave Gate to be developed. In 1935, the City

St Leonard's Terrace in the 1960s. This terrace was at the end of Grundon Street and overlooked the River Soar. There was only a footpath between the front of these houses and the river bank. Grundon Street was off Abbey Gate and was originally in quite a rural setting. These houses would have been far superior to the slums closer to the centre of town. Today the site of these cottages is to the east of the junction of St Margaret's Way and Ravensbridge Road. Grundon Street Bridge across the river to St Margaret's pasture still survives.

Surveyor brought forward an ambitious plan for a new dual carriageway, similar to Charles Street. This was a bypass designed to relieve congestion at the Clock Tower and in the High Street. Running from Foundry Lane to Great Central Street, by way of Burley's Lane and Archdeacon Lane, it cut across a big area of slum property. On one side of it, close to Abbey Street, a new bus station would be built and Abbey Street itself widened. Although St Margaret's bus station was under construction at the outbreak of war, Burley's Way and Vaughan Way had made little progress and were not completed until the 1960s.

During 1938 the clearance of Leicester's slums reached its height. By the year's end sanitary inspectors were diverted away from slum clearance to air raid precautions; surveying cellars for shelters and equipping first aid posts. The rearmament programme also caused the government to cut the housing subsidy, wiping out the effect of the fall in interest rates. When war was declared, the planned re-housing of the residents of Wharf Street was halted and the war effort brought work on housing to a virtual standstill by 1940. By then over 3,500 houses had been demolished and 2,859 replacements built. It was another 14 years before the programme was restarted.

In 1942, work was begun by the City Council on a plan for post-war reconstruction. There was much publicity, including an exhibition and a report which was published in 1944. This work was to form the basis for post-war slum clearance and redevelopment over the next 20 years. However, the city faced a severe housing shortage at the end of the war and the need was to build new houses, rather than replace existing ones. In 1949, the

Above: St Leonard's Cottages in Bradgate Street looking from Diamond Street to Bradgate Street, May 1963. This little group of streets off Woodgate included Diamond Street, Crystal Street, Opal Street and Littleton Street, and they had all been laid out by the Leicester architect William Millican in 1872.

Medical Officer of Health commented that the housing situation was the most serious concern to public health. There was a need for 20,000 houses but only 749 had been built. The 1951 census showed that there were still 12,200 houses without an internal water supply, 17,300 with shared outside WCs and even 73 houses with pail closets. There were hundreds of houses in areas which had been declared clearance areas in the mid-1930s but were still occupied 10 years later.

However, the swift progress of the New Parks estate began to ease the situation and slum clearance returned to the Council's agenda. During 1950, health inspectors, diverted away from their usual work, began to resurvey the city with a view to restarting clearance. In what must have been a huge effort, they surveyed around 20,000 houses and by 1951 the Medical Officer of Health's team had identified 18,429 houses which were unfit and should be demolished within the next 20 years. This report, coupled with incentives from central government, spurred the resumption of slum clearance in Leicester, and the Council adopted an ambitious target of clearing 12,000 houses. However, this long-term plan drew criticism from estate agents. They felt that property which might be demolished in the final 10 years of the plan in Highfields might become blighted in the short-term. However, there were also reports of people buying 'slums' in the hope of being rehoused by the Council.

At the end of 1952, Lewin Street became the first post-war clearance area. With 247 houses, it was thought to be the largest clearance area in the country at that time. Lewin Street was part of the Wharf Street development area which comprised 1,182 houses. Out of these 739 had no internal water supply and 1,048 had no separate toilet. By the end of 1957, over 2,000 houses had been demolished.

To implement this ambitious programme, all the major committee chairs were drawn

Above: Bradgate Street, looking towards Abbey Gate, being demolished in May 1965. These two-bedroom houses were built in 1873 and were of a better standard of construction than many other houses previously demolished. They were probably classified as unfit because of rising damp, inadequate bathrooms and thin brickwork at the rear. (Author)

together to oversee the work under Labour's leading local politician, Charles Keene. He had led the post-war reconstruction committee from 1946 and chaired the new committee, responsible for clearance and redevelopment, from 1956 until the late 1960s. His vice-chair, Ken Bowder, a Conservative, had an even longer period of office and their co-operation reflected the political consensus over slum clearance. The clearance programme was to continue under both Labour and Conservative administrations until the mid-1970s.

At that time, Leicester's slum clearance programme was more advanced than many other comparable cities and by 1965 Leicester had cleared 8,351 slum houses, which was more than Liverpool but less than Birmingham and Leeds.[3] As the programme started, there was concern that people who lived in unfit housing should not be stigmatised with the word 'slum'. Cllr May Goodwin, who was chairman of the Housing Committee, felt the best way to achieve this was by ensuring that people from clearance areas were rehoused throughout the housing stock rather than being confined to a particular estate. However, these good intentions were subsequently undermined by the difference in rent levels between pre- and post-war Council housing. The older pre-war housing estates had lower rents and inevitably many poor people chose these houses out of necessity.

During the mid-1930s leading Conservatives had advocated the building of flats in Leicester for slum dwellers, but the majority of the Council remained wedded to the garden suburb approach. It was felt that the Council was forcing people to live on the outskirts of

---

3. Apart from London, only Birmingham, Manchester, Liverpool and Stoke had demolished more houses.

With no hot tap, this sink may not look luxurious, but even in the 1950s there were still a few houses without an internal sink or water supply. (Author)

the city and there was a belief that people should have the choice to stay in the centre of town if they wanted. However, the cost of land in the central areas was prohibitive – 10 times the price of land on New Parks. It was for this reason that the Labour Group abandoned the previous policy of cottage homes and supported the building of tenement-style blocks on the first phase of the St Matthew's estate. The Conservatives eventually opposed the building of housing there, instead wanting the whole area to be given over to industrial development and topped by a 'helicopter station'. They were outvoted. Flats soon became the norm for the inner-city estates of St Peter's, St Mark's and St Andrew's. The use of unconventional designs, layouts and construction methods was later to be a matter of concern on some of these estates.

It has been suggested that in the 1950s, the Conservatives favoured improvement rather than demolition.[4] However, the view of Cllr Ken Bowder was quite plain when he said in 1957, 'I think we all agree that the slums cannot come down too quickly.' In 1955, the Conservatives argued that the Council should temporarily patch up those houses which would not be demolished for another five years or more. They felt that families should not be forced to endure appalling conditions while they waited to be rehoused. However, Labour argued that clearing and replacing sub-standard housing was already stretching the Council's resources to the limit and to patch up old houses as well would only further delay building new ones. The long wait for new buildings was blamed on the government reduction in new homes for Leicester from 1,500 to 1,000.

From 1954, the Conservative government had recycled its pre-war housing policy and reduced and then cut housing subsidy for any other Council housing other than slum

4. Ben Beazley, *Postwar Leicester*. In 1954, the Conservatives had proposed the Council should modernise two properties in an effort to encourage landlords to apply for grants. They did not offer this as an alternative to clearance.

A cupboard used for food storage in a house in Willow Street. The problem of poor food storage, highlighted by Tom Barclay in the 1890s, was still an issue 60 years later. The packet of Surf dates this picture to after 1953. (Author)

clearance. It was thought that the private sector would meet the need. Up to 1961 the Council was building 1,000 homes a year, which was then reduced to about 800. Cuts in the new building programme caused problems. The Council struggled to find enough homes for the large numbers of families, while the redevelopment of cleared sites was not keeping in step with clearance. As a result there were large areas of town where boarded up houses or vacant lots had become significant eyesores. After 1966, the clearance programme was reduced to 600 houses per year.

Although there were occasional proposals from back-bench Councillors favouring the improvement of old property, it was argued that landlords made such a policy impossible. Grants were available for landlords, but the uptake was miniscule. May Goodwin's view in 1960 was that landlords were only interested in collecting the rent, not installing baths. Renovating old houses on the existing street layouts would have also prevented the Council's road plans for the development of car parks, new schools and sites for industry.

By the mid-1960s many of the houses and neighbourhoods scheduled for demolition were no longer the insanitary back-to-backs and courtyards which had been cleared in the 1930s, but were bye-law housing in poor repair with damp problems and inadequate bathrooms. By earlier standards, these houses would have been thought of as being quite superior. In 1966, the Council adopted an area-based programme of requiring landlords to improve properties so tenants had the five basic amenities. In 1969, the idea that older terraced housing could be improved found favour when a 'general improvement area' was introduced in Clarendon Park. This policy still ran in tandem with slum clearance, and house demolitions continued at around the rate of 500 per year.

The replacement of the terraces of Wharf Street with the flats of St Matthew's had been controversial in the 1950s. The comprehensive development plans adopted by the Council for new roads, industrial areas and housing meant that the road patterns had to be changed. With the development of new roads like Burley's Way and later Waterloo Way, whole streets were destined to disappear without trace. In the Charnwood Street area, it was not possible to build new houses and facilities on the existing street pattern and so some existing streets disappeared. In some cases, sound houses were compulsorily purchased and demolished in order to facilitate this kind of redevelopment. The demolition of unfit housing and their replacement by new Council housing had undoubtedly improved health and mortality rates. However, house demolition also became an instrument for road building, constructing car parks and 'modernisation'.

Braunstone Park was the home of the 82nd Airborne Division prior to the D-Day landings in 1944. At the end of the war, homeless people in different parts of the country began to take over abandoned military camps. These occupations forced the government to allow the camps to be used for temporary housing. The Braunstone Park camp was used by the City Council to house displaced families until permanent homes could be found. With such a housing shortage, no slum clearance was possible until more homes could be built. (Leicester Mercury)

By the mid-1970s, the plans for clearance drawn up in the 1950s were all but complete. At the end of 1976 some 12,500 houses had been demolished, leaving only Martin Street and Laurel Road to be cleared. Ken Middleton, who was vicar of St Matthew's and leader of the Council, had bitterly regretted the demolition of Leicester's 'Petticoat Lane' in Charnwood Street. A new generation of Councillors and officers were beginning to work out a strategy for renewing existing housing that was basically sound. The removal of thriving communities to make way for high-rise replacements had become less popular with the public. Road schemes, which came on the back of slum clearance, also met with growing opposition. In the West End, structurally sound housing was compulsory purchased during 1970–71 to enable 'outworn terraces' to be cleared. This allowed road works for an improved western approach to the city along the A47 and King Richard's Road. As public opposition to new roads grew, plans for an Eastern Relief Road through South Highfields faltered and were eventually abandoned.

This was all brought to a head with the threatened demolition of Bartholomew, Myrtle and Biddulph Streets. In 1968, these 165 houses had been scheduled for improvement. By 1974, most had not been improved and so were put in a clearance area. In 1975, Shelter argued that these streets should be improved and not demolished. With a decline in the building of new housing, Shelter was concerned the demand was outstripping supply. Local residents and Councillors, like Peter Soulsby, believed that these houses would have a useful life once they were improved. Their voices were influential in the Labour Group and in January 1976 the Council agreed to renovate the Bartholomew Street area.

This picture from the early 1950s shows Mrs Pethers and her three children, Terence (11), Michael (4) and Averil (2), in the cheerless, sunless yard which provided the only access to her house and the only place where the children could play. Behind is the window of the living room which let in so little light that the electric light had to be left on all day. (Leicester Mercury)

In April 1976, the Council agreed a new policy for older housing. The first stated aim was to 'put an end to the wholesale disturbance of people and the breaking up of natural communities by improving houses instead of demolishing them.' The second was to encourage more private investment in older houses. The city was divided up into 54 zones, covering about 35,000 houses which were to be improved during the period 1976 to 1991 using renovation grants. Although renewal rather than clearance was now the preferred approach to poor housing, in June 1978 there were still 362 unfit houses left from the clearance programme awaiting demolition. (These were, for the most part, located in Martin Street.)

Even today, the stigma implied in the word slum is still with us. The roots of that stigma lay in the philosophy behind the Poor Law which laid the blame for poverty on its victims. While Joseph Dare's reports emphasise the importance of the environment, his reports did not evade moralising. In the 1850s and 1860s, he maintained that decency and morality could not prosper in the unhealthy surrounding of the slums. In his view, they could only foster crime, drunkenness and depravity. With children of different sexes sharing bedrooms or sleeping in their parents' room, overcrowding was seen by him as the first step towards sexual licence. Despite the grim conditions, the slums are not described as either evil or sordid by many of those who remember them

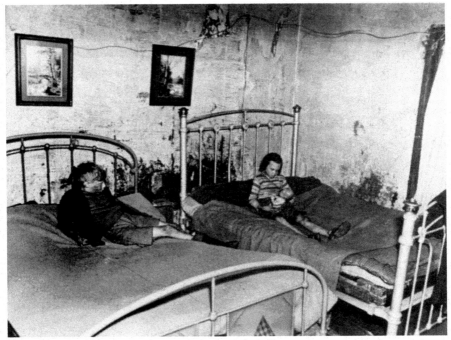

In 1951, five people slept in this bedroom at No. 22 Warrington Street. This two-roomed house was occupied by Mr and Mrs Frank Smith and their three children. Two girls aged 14 and nine and a boy aged 11 slept in the bed on the right, and their parents used the one on the left. Warrington Street ran parallel to Northgate Street between Pingle Street and Soar Lane, and the 178 houses in the area were demolished sometime after 1956. The street has now virtually disappeared. (Leicester Mercury)

first-hand. Those who grew up in these districts are keen to point to the community spirit and neighbourliness which characterised these tightly knit communities. Given that so many people lived in enclosed yards, sharing toilets and taps, this is hardly surprising.

Today we value our old buildings. Demolition proposals are often frustrated by determined opposition and we now scorn those who in the past allowed the destruction of what we think of as our heritage. The demolition of unfit housing and their replacement by new Council buildings had undoubtedly improved health and mortality rates. However, would slum clearance have continued into the 1970s had the technology of injected damp-proof courses been adopted earlier? Charles Keene's concept of comprehensive redevelopment led to changes which went far beyond slum clearance. To understand why so much of what we now think of as historic has disappeared, we need to get into the mindset of those who believed in progress and modernity and were not sentimental about old buildings. To them, the past meant the squalid and unhealthy conditions in which many of them had grown up. Spacious Council houses with kitchens, bathrooms, decent sanitation and gardens were the future. On top of this was the desire to turn a Victorian city into one which could accommodate new industry and the motor car. In this context the obsession with all things modern was understandable and slum clearance had made it easier for people to believe that new meant better.

'Conditions such as exist in this Leicester slum kitchen appal most people, but nothing has been done,' said the Illustrated Leicester Chronicle *in April 1952.* (Leicester Mercury)

In 1956, the chairman of the Planning Committee, Councillor A.N. Vesty, proposed the demolition of the 120-year-old Theatre Royal in Horsefair Street, saying that he would be 'surprised to hear of anyone wanting to preserve the building on the grounds of architectural merit'. Councillor Arthur Marriot went further when he described it as 'a monstrosity in line with the town hall'. When, a year later, Cllr Vesty moved for the demolition of William Carey's historic cottage in Thornton Lane, which stood in the way of the ring road, only one Councillor voted against. In 1966, the decision was made to demolish the Bell Hotel and redevelop the Haymarket with car parks, a civic theatre and pedestrian arcades.

The legacy of slum clearance is still very much in evidence. It is to be seen in comfortable post-war estates on the outskirts of the city, which have provided thousands with a level of amenity that would have been inconceivable to their forbears. However, the scattering of car parks and utilitarian industrial and commercial buildings on the sites of the slums in the inner city is less than impressive. Although Conrad Smigelski, the city's former planning officer, is now held to account for the cumulative effects of 1960s planning on Leicester, many of the insensitive and destructive side effects of road plans predate his appointment in 1962. The destruction of Leicester's mediaeval street plan by the completion of the ring road had been planned years before by his predecessor John Beckett.

Britain has long been an unequal society. The slums were a very visible manifestation of that inequality and their clearance came at a time when people wanted to narrow the gap between rich and poor. Recent governments have reverted to the belief that private

According to the Illustrated Leicester Chronicle *in August 1951, 11 people lived in this house.* (Leicester Mercury)

enterprise is better able to meet people's social needs and have worshiped the power of the market. However, it is worth noting that the squalor of slum housing was the net result of unfettered enterprise, the consequences of which were only belatedly dealt with by the intervention of a public sector accountable to the town hall and parliament. Although slum clearance greatly improved housing conditions, it did not remove inequality and poverty. Although the population of St Matthew's estate has changed significantly, it remains the most deprived neighbourhood in Leicester. A 2007 survey showed that, on the basis of income, it was the poorest area in England.

Although thousands of people lived in Leicester's slum areas, the historical record is very uneven. No plans of working-class housing built before 1849 survive. Subsequently, the Council only needed floor plans and it is only towards the end of the 19th century that detailed plans were required. Photographic evidence is also patchy: by some quirk of fate, there is a better photographic record of the streets demolished in the 1930s than of those demolished in the 1960s. Many of the pictures in this book were taken by the Council's

Garton Place ran off Joseph Street, which in turn ran parallel to Walnut Street. The large building in the background is the Crown buildings on Walnut Street. This pleasant courtyard layout can still be seen today on Gordon, Woodbine, College and Oxford Avenues in South Highfields. (Newarke Houses Museum)

health officers while areas were being surveyed for future clearance. They were usually taken when the houses were still being lived in.

The Leicester artist John Flowers established the honourable tradition of recording buildings threatened with demolition in the 1830s. Over 100 years later photographers followed suit, taking pictures shortly before or during demolition; often when the local residents had moved out and the houses were boarded up and the streets empty of people. As far as possible I have excluded this type of picture from this book, since, although they faithfully record the street layout and the dilapidation of the buildings, they show nothing of the bustle of life that existed in these teeming districts. Hopefully, the written accounts can give a glimpse of the vitality that is sometimes absent from photographs of decaying brickwork and empty streets.

The city we now inhabit is a very different place to the forgotten streets pictured in this book. For younger people and for the many others, like me, who did not arrive in Leicester until the 1970s, our picture of the past is often formed by what has survived. With many 19th-century homes of the wealthy and better off still much in evidence, this can be misleading. As memories of the old communities in the slums fade, it is natural that we might forget how and where poor people lived. This book is therefore an attempt to provide a more democratic understanding of our city's past.

Ned Newitt, February 2009

This engraved street map of Leicester was commissioned by the Council's Highways and Sewerage Committee in 1851 and was seen as a vital tool in the cause of 'sanitary reform'. It appeared in the Medical Officer's annual reports and was used to show the spread of disease in the town. Other maps document deaths from scarlet fever, measles, smallpox and diphtheria. This map also shows the extent of housing in Leicester prior to the 1859 building bye-laws, much of which constituted Leicester's slum districts.

Leicester

Angus Reach, The Morning Chronicle, *1849.*
In 1841, Angus Reach was appointed as parliamentary reporter for the Morning Chronicle. *The post had previously been held by Charles Dickens. In 1849, Henry Mayhew suggested that the* Morning Chronicle *should carry out an investigation into the condition of the labouring classes in England and Wales. The editor agreed and recruited a team that included Angus Reach:*

The town of Leicester lies in a gentle hollow, sheltered, except towards the east, by the undulations of the Dane and Spinney hills. The sluggish stream of the Soar winds through the town; and in wet weather the adjacent meadows are swampy and often overflowed. The consequence is, the frequent prevalence of fever in the lowest-lying portions of the town. The mean duration of life in England is 29.11 years. In Leicester it is 25 years. The drainage is miserably defective. Out of 242 streets and 3,417 courts, alleys and yards, only 112 are entirely culverted, and about 130 partially so. There are nine outfalls of sewers, all situated in the town, and all pouring their contents into the most stagnant waters of the Soar. The surface drainage is equally defective. There is seldom sufficient fall to carry away the dirty water. At the back of each block of the more ordinary class of houses is a common yard, with privies, cesspools and ash-pits, for the use of the occupants. From these places there is seldom or never any sub-soil drainage. Slops and liquid refuse are left to evaporate, and send up their noisome effluvia. Of the 13,991 houses in Leicester only 120 are supplied with water closets – the average cost of each being £31 10s, a sum equal to half the amount necessary for building a four-roomed house. Many of the cesspools are of great depth; some of them not less than 25ft; and the consequence is that, in numerous instances, the water which is found still nearer the surface is poisoned by noxious percolations.

Report of the Inspector of Nuisances

George Bown (1770–1858), Hall Book, 7 October 1846.
In the 1790s, George Bown was the secretary of the Constitutional Society for Promoting the Equal Representation of the People in Parliament and signed a manifesto demanding complete suffrage. With Richard Phillips, he founded the Leicester Herald *in 1792 and in 1794 he was briefly arrested for his Jacobin sympathies. For many years he was book keeper to the 'Hope' coach at the Bell Hotel.*
Following the passing of the Reform Bill in 1831, he became clerk to the Reform Society which was at the heart of the Radical-Whig alliance. When this alliance came to power on the Council in 1835, he was appointed as the receiver of flour returns and as an accountant. In the early 1840s Bown was the first editor of the Leicester Chartist paper the Midland Counties Illuminator. *Thomas Cooper described him as a 'fine intellectual old man, whose pamphlets, fly-sheets and contributions to periodicals would fill many volumes if collected'. In 1846, aged 76, he became the Council's Inspector of Nuisances and in the extract below, he describes some of the various threats to public health and proposes that the Council should appoint paid Medical Officers of Health. The proposal was accepted and as a result Leicester became the first local authority to have such officers. Bown retired in 1849.*

I have to report to the Council a special communication of the most flagrant nuisances which call for more immediate remedy. Independent of the following, there is scarcely a courtyard, alley or narrow street, particularly in the lower parts of the town, that has not

BOROUGH OF   LEICESTER

PUBLIC HEALTH ACT.

NOTICE IS HEREBY GIVEN,

That in consequence of "The Public Health Act 1848" (11 and 12 Vic. c. 63) having been applied to the Borough of Leicester, the following provisions of such Act are now in operation within this Borough, and will be enforced by the Local Board of Health.

NEW BUILDINGS.

It shall not be lawful newly to erect any House, or to rebuild any House which may have been pulled down to or below the ground floor, or to occupy any House so newly erected or rebuilt until a covered drain be constructed of such size and materials, and at such level, and with such fall as, upon the Report of the Surveyor to the Local Board, shall appear to be necessary and sufficient for the efficient drainage of the same and its appurtenances; and any person erecting or rebuilding any House, or constructing any drain, contrary to this enactment, is liable to a penalty of FIFTY POUNDS, (11 and 12 Vic., c. 63, s. 49.) Fourteen days at the least before beginning to dig or lay out the foundations for any new House, or to rebuild any House pulled down to the ground floor, the person intending so to build, or rebuild, must give written notice thereof to the Local Board, stating the intended level of the cellars or lowest floor, and the situation and construction of the Privies and Cesspools to be built or used in connexion with such House, where a penalty of FIFTY POUNDS: and the Local Board may cause any House, Privy, or Cesspool, built without their approval of the above particulars, to be altered or pulled down at the expence of the offender, (11 and 12 Vic., c. 63, s. 53.) To enable them to determine upon the above matters, the Local Board require a Ground Plan, shewing the whole of the premises, with a section and cross section of the same, the datum line of the section being the kirb stone in the street, adjoining the premises at the spot where the drainage is intended to fall into the gutter or culvert, to be sent in with the Notice.

NEW STREETS.

One month at least before any Street is newly laid out, written notice must be given to the Local Board of Health, shewing the intended level and width thereof, and the level and width are to be fixed by the Local Board, with a power of appeal to the General Board; and any person laying out, making, or building upon such Street otherwise than in accordance with the level and width fixed by the Local Board, or approved by the General Board, is liable to a penalty of TWENTY POUNDS for every day during which he shall under such Street to continue to laid out, made, or built upon, (11 and 12 Vic. c. 63, s. 72.)

ALL NOTICES or particulars required under the foregoing enactments may be delivered at the Accountants Office at the Town Hall, being the Office of the Local Board.

BY ORDER,
SAMUEL STONE,
Clerk to the Local Board of Health.

Leicester, October 4th, 1849.

WINKS, PRINTER, LEICESTER.

BOROUGH OF   LEICESTER

PUBLIC HEALTH ACT.

NOTICE IS HEREBY GIVEN,

That in consequence of "The Public Health Act 1848" (11 and 12 Vic. c. 63) having been applied to the Borough of Leicester, the following provisions of such Act are now in operation within this Borough, and will be enforced by the Local Board of Health.

COMMON LODGING-HOUSES.

Every person keeping, or intending to keep any Common Lodging House within this Borough is required forthwith to register his name and the situation of his house, at the Town Hall Library, where a Register Book is kept for this purpose; and any person receiving lodgers in any Common Lodging House, without having registered the same, is liable for every offence to a penalty of FORTY SHILLINGS. (11 and 12 Vic. c. 63, s. 66.)

SLAUGHTER-HOUSES.

The owner or occupier of every building or place used as a Slaughter House within this Borough is required forthwith to register his name and the situation of his premises at the Town Hall Library, where a Register Book is kept for this purpose, on or before the First day of November next; and any person who shall use, or suffer to be used, any building or place as a Slaughter House without its being so registered, is liable to a penalty of FIVE POUNDS. (11 and 12 Vic. c. 63, s. 61.) And the business of a Slaughterer of Cattle, Horses, or Animals of any description, may not be newly established in any building or place, after the First day of August last, without the consent of the Town Council or the Local Board of Health, under a penalty of FIFTY POUNDS. (11 and 12 Vic. c. 63, s. 61.)

OFFENSIVE TRADES.

The business of a Blood-boiler, Bone-boiler, Fellmonger, Slaughterer of Cattle, Horses, or Animals of any description, Soap-boiler, Tallow-melter, Tripe-boiler, or other noxious or offensive business, trade, or manufacture, shall not be newly established in any building or place within the said Borough after the first day of August last, without the consent of the Town Council as the Local Board of Health, (unless the General Board shall otherwise direct); and whoever offends against this enactment is liable to a penalty of FIFTY POUNDS. (11 and 12 Vic. c. 63, s. 61.)

ALL NOTICES or particulars required under the foregoing enactments may be delivered at the Accountants Office at the Town Hall, being the Office of the Local Board.

BY ORDER,
SAMUEL STONE,
Clerk to the Local Board of Health.

Leicester, October 4th, 1849.

WINKS, PRINTER, LEICESTER.

Although these 1849 posters were produced under the authority of the 1848 Health Act, they give effect to the proposals for bye-laws made by Drs Buck and Barclay in 1847.

its accumulation of filth to an extent highly prejudicial and dangerous to its inhabitants and the neighbourhood.

The narrow ditch at the right-hand side of the lower end of Belgrave Gate is the common recipient of the large culverts descending from Granby Street and the Humberstone Gate and Road; they here unite and their contents are openly exposed for at least 90 yards before the ditch passes under the Turnpike Road and empties itself into the canal basin. Although this nuisance lies at the very extremity of the town, when the wind blows from an easterly quarter its noisome exhalations are perceptible almost to the cross. I should say that a more pestiferous and dangerous nuisance does not exist in the town...

Two sheds in Mansfield Street with coppers and low chimneys in which the half-putrid fragments from two slaughterhouses are cooked weekly, to the extreme annoyance of the neighbourhood and to the danger of the health of whoever in passing may inhale their effluvia. Frith, the nightman, has an open repository for night soil etc which has been repeatedly and hitherto unavailingly complained of by the neighbours and has been recently testified, by qualified medical practitioners, as having been the cause of fever thereabout. Knight, the scavenger, has a receptacle of a similar character in Bedford Street, which is certified as being prejudicial to the health of the inhabitants residing in contact with it in the surrounding areas...

In the more crowded parts of the town the frequent close contiguity of slaughterhouses, pigsties and privies, the latter too with walls seldom more than 3ft in height, are a perpetual source of visitation: the poisonous exhalations from which, having no chance of escape, even in the brisk winds, the surrounding houses form a kind of cistern of concentrated contamination, never wholly dispersed, and which is not easy to dilute or dissipate.

Unfortunately, these three photographs have no inscription to indicate a time or place. The Swithland slate over the entry on the house suggests that this is an older part of Leicester. These courtyard houses were tucked away far from the street and the whitewash was an attempt to provide light in what must have often been a dark yard. Despite some gentile dilapidation, this secluded courtyard seems cared for and cosy. (Author)

Left: The rear of Nos 18–32 St John Street (near St Margaret's Church) in the late 1930s. This view is from the Luke Street end of the common yard in which there was one tap and four WCs for the joint use of the eight houses. Nos 18 to 24 were hemmed in by the tall buildings of what was, in 1888, the London Steam Crane and Engine Works. The demolition workman on the left is standing at the entrance to the covered passage to St John Street. The windows are taped for fumigation. (Author)

Below: The rear of Nos 4–16 St John Street seen from Burley's Lane looking towards Luke Street. The factory chimney belongs to what became the British United shoe machinery factory. The other side of this factory can be seen in the photograph above.

Medical Sanitary Officers' Report

Dr John Barclay and Dr John Buck, Hall Book, 24 February 1847.
John Buck and John Barclay were appointed as the town's medical officers in 1846. Their appointment enabled the sometimes controversial decisions requiring the closure of houses or slaughterhouses to be cloaked in the authority of professional expertise. Their medical status enabled them to propose new bye-laws in their very first report, reproduced in part below.

The district by far the most fertile in nuisances prejudicial to the health of the inhabitants has been the lower part of the Parish of St Margaret's, and particularly the streets and courts to the eastwards of Wharf Street. The older streets at the upper part of Belgrave Gate, the streets and yards to the northward of the Sanvey Gate and the district called the Friars have also furnished a large proportion of cases for medical certificates.

The palpable source of the fever, which raged during the autumn, has been the nuisance arising from the evaporation of the foul water which inundated certain parts of town during the summer floods, by which the filth from the large sewers was carried back into many houses, yards and streets at the lower part of Belgrave Gate and Archdeacon Lane.

But the nuisance which seems to your medical officers to call most imperatively for immediate remedy is the very universal practice of keeping pigs in or near dwellings in the borough. The pigsties invariably give rise to the most intolerable stenches in their immediate vicinity and those that keep them are tempted to keep in great quantity their manure and all sorts of refuse from the streets and elsewhere for sale; thus forming, as we judge, the foci of disease on a very extensive scale.

The numerous small slaughterhouses, to which the last mentioned nuisance in some small measure gives rise, also appears to be very objectionable, as in many instances the blood and offal has to be swilled down some distance on the open street before a covered drain can be reached; and frequently this cleansing is totally neglected or very inefficiently performed.

Before making any particular suggestions we would express our decided opinion of the prime necessity of a complete system of drainage, flushing and trapping for this town, without which it is in vain to expect to raise its mean duration of life to that of the United Kingdom.

In the first instance, we would recommend a bye-law prohibiting pigs being kept in the borough within 30 to 40ft of any human dwelling. Second, we would prohibit night soil being collected in yards in the borough. Third, some means by which the frequent periodical emptying of cesspools and privy-holes may be enforced. Fourth, that where the defective formation of streets causes water to be accumulated, some means be found to carry it off [and] no new streets to be built without proper drains. Fifth, that stench traps be placed on gully holes of the drains and the public streets of the borough.

A Letter to the Chairman of the Highways and Sewerage Committee

John Buck, Officer of Health, 10 November 1852.

You, sir, are well aware that at present almost all the plans for cottages are presented with cesspool arrangements for their privies; the tendency being, I fear, to bring them nearer and nearer to the houses themselves, thus poisoning the air and water in the neighbourhood. Now so firmly convinced am I of the enormous amount of mischief caused by these mal-arrangements, of the many maladies rendered malignant and fatal by the detention of decaying material among living persons, that I feel a perfect abhorrence at the idea of being

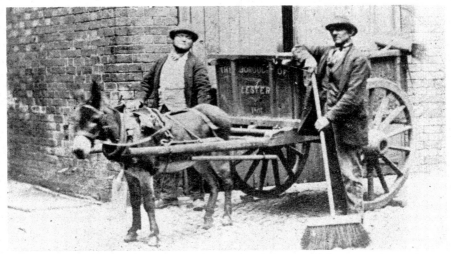

An undated picture of the town's street cleaners or 'scavengers'. The inscription on the cart reads: 'The Borough of Lester 1867'. This work, like that of emptying privies, was contracted out.

called upon to sanction a single cesspool more in the town. The statistics of infant mortality...all point most clearly to our cesspool system as the chief cause of this fatality...Imbued with these feelings, I dislike sanctioning one year, what I feel impelled next year to remove.

The Collection, Disposal and Utilisation of Town Refuse in Leicester

F.W. Allen, Assistant Borough Surveyor, Leicester, 5 December 1903.
The disposal of sewage was perhaps even more primitive than the water supply. The privy midden was the most obnoxious feature of 19th-century slums. Usually, there was one privy midden to each court, which consisted of a seat over a brick receptacle or unlined cesspit into which household ashes and rubbish were also thrown. The contents of the cesspit frequently seeped out, contaminating wells or overflowing when not emptied regularly.

By the 1850s, a fair number of middle-class houses had water closets, but these were unknown to the working classes. Their spread was held back by the refusal of the Waterworks Company to supply water for a WC unless water was also taken for household use. Such a water supply would also be expensive. Before the introduction of pail closets in the 1870s, the Council concentrated its public health efforts on getting landlords to replace leaking and noxious cesspits with privy vaults, which had a watertight lining to keep the sewage from seeping out. The passage below was written at a time when the replacement of pail closets had begun to improve public health.

Being an old walled town, its streets were narrow and tortuous, and paved with cobbles and pebbles. Its houses were crowded, its yards confined in area and paved, where paved at all, with pebbles. A total lack of proper sewerage; the abominable privy system in full swing with all its offensive appendages of deep, open, reeking cesspool or covered vault; open, deep manure pits; a water supply, obtained for the most part from shallow surface wells

This photograph is thought to be of Frog Island in the early 1870s. It might well show the construction of the Evans Weir, looking towards the houses built at the rear of All Saints Road near the Jarvis Street Corporation depot. The building of the weirs and the Mile Straight did much to reduce flooding in the town.

placed, as usual, in close proximity to the cesspools; no proper system of refuse removal, the farmers attending to the cesspools, vaults etc when it suited them best (their leaky wagons frequently leaving a filthy ill-smelling trail through the streets after the night's work); these were the environments of the Leicester man 50 years ago.

Thus it came about that during the hot months of July and August, when the diarrhoea scourge would be at its height, the town was in the most unhealthy condition. There were also, in the oldest and most densely populated parts of the town, no fewer than 104 slaughterhouses (one to every 600 persons), with large open cesspools or manure-pits, on which pigs were kept in some instances for the consumption of blood and offal. Many of the slaughterhouses were without any drains whatever, the scourings of their yards being traceable over undrained and badly paved streets for a considerable distance before finding an exit by a more or less direct route through the old shallow box drains, which did duty as sewers, into the river.

At a moderate computation, therefore, there must have been an area of reeking

These one up, one down cottages at the rear of Dannett Street were built in the 1860s on land purchased by the Freehold Land Society. The estate was originally laid out with ample gardens, which were soon crammed with intervening rows of cottages with no road frontage. (see Joseph Dare, opposite)

filth equal to something like three acres. There is no record of street cleansing in those days; but some years later the cleansing was let to working contractors, who usually worked a whole district with a small cart and a patient donkey. Add to this the fact that July floods very often covered a considerable portion of the built area in the West End, leaving a filthy deposit of mud in streets and dwellings, and it is clear that the death rate of 24.9 per 1,000 (a percentage of 29.5 under one year of age) was, under the circumstances, not to be wondered at.

Report of the Leicester Domestic Mission

Joseph Dare, 1864.
The Unitarian social missionary Joseph Dare made yearly reports between 1846 and 1877 on the condition of working-class life in Leicester.

I have ascertained that there are at least 1,000 dwellings in this town that have neither back doors nor windows. So that allowing five inmates to each, which will be found under the mark, as the lower the grade of the population the thicker is the crowding together, there are no less than between seven and eight thousand sweltering in these wretched unhealthy abodes. The habits, too, of the inmates of backyards and confined courts are altogether different from those who live in sunlight and fresh air. Seldom seen by respectable people, they are heedless both of personal appearance and domestic cleanliness. From the common use of the same filthy 'midden' and vulgar familiarities among themselves, gossiping in common at each other's houses, they lose all decency of manners and sink into both moral and physical corruption. Hence it will be seen that moral causes have much to do with the sanitary condition of towns. In addition to scarlatina, typhus fever and measles, it is also well known that smallpox spreads its fearful ravages widely among us.

In the course of my visits, I had necessarily to call on many afflicted with this loathsome disease. All the cases I met with were in very close dwellings, some of them without back openings, and the others apparently over-crowded, as in one house I found four grown-up persons who suffered from it, the father dying; in another confined dwelling four had it, three of them adults; in another house with no back ventilation, four children died. I never before found so many ill of this terrible malady. The impression among many was that this disease was brought to the town in the leather. Most likely this idea arose from the fact that several shoemakers were among its first victims. And this fact shows that personal habits have much to do with the origination of the disease, for with grief it must be stated this class are among the most degraded of the working population.

Report of the Leicester Domestic Mission

Joseph Dare, 1872.

Our confined courts are the nurseries of vice, disease and death. They are becoming more and more so from year to year. The greater number of these places when first built were open on some sides to the 'breath of heaven'. Leicester was formerly noted for gardens and intra-mural spaces; these are fast disappearing. Yards and courts are being more closely surrounded, overshadowed by factories and blank walls, till the very air and sunlight are excluded as not belonging to our common humanity. Think of 30 or 40 individuals using the same recess, and this dammed up at the back with the filth and refuse of a number of dwellings without back doors or windows, and placed only a few feet from the entrances to these 'Mount Pleasants', or 'Spring Gardens', or 'Paradise Rows', as the case may be. I know that many of these sinks have not been emptied during the whole of the summer. I could point to wholesale smallpox in one yard, to consumption in another, to baby mortality in a third and to measles and scarlatina everywhere. While our present insanitary condition continues, our Councillors, instead of erecting ornamental and official buildings at enormous cost, should lay out the sums in the purchase and demolition of these lurking places of pestilence and immorality.

It is discouraging to observe that in several of the newly built parts of the town, as between Flora Street and Clara Street on King Richard's Road, and other localities, there are inter-buildings springing up between the streets as originally laid out. Rows of small scamped tenements approached from the main street, through narrow arched passages, choke up what ought to be gardens and breathing spaces and completely destroy the comfort and convenience, to say nothing of the health, of the first possessors. Each row so inter-built necessarily confines the backs of itself and at least two other rows of houses. The land as at first laid out was not intended to be thus glutted up by an inferior class of dwellings. I know some who bought and built upon it with this understanding. All this is very bad; and if our 'bye-laws' sanction such crowding of habitations, so much the worse for the bye-laws, which in this respect must be amended, or the town will still be notorious for its unhealthy condition.

Report of the Medical Officer of Health

J. Wyatt Crane MD, 1867 and 1874.
In the days before Pasteur's concept of germs had become established, the cause of Leicester's high infant mortality rate from diarrhoea was hotly debated. Was it caused by gas from the sewers or the failure of working women to breastfeed? In 1868, the local Board of Health believed the cause of these deaths lay in the existence of open privy cesspools in the town. This view was not shared by Dr Crane. He steadfastly refused to accept that diarrhoea was a Zymotic disease (caused by germs) linked to the insanitary state of the poorer districts. This was a fatal error of judgement. In 1902, one of Crane's successors, Dr Killick Millard, conducted a survey which concluded that the reason poor women were unable to breastfeed was not because of work, but because they were unable to produce enough milk.

I believe that the increase in the cases of diarrhoea in Leicester will be found to depend more upon the increase of its manufacturers, and the consequent diversion of a greater

A common ashpit and pail closet side by side in Taylor Street.

number of mothers from the congenial occupation of nursing their own children to manufacturing labours, than to any special cause: the natural result being that children are fed upon food unsuited to them; that they manifest their pain and injury to their health which it causes by their constant fretfulness and crying; and to soothe the excitement which they produce in their guardians, are dosed with 'godfrey' or laudanum to keep them quiet.

Can we wonder that these pallid emaciated children...fall victim of diarrhoea easily set up in the languor of the system produced by the heats of autumn days followed by the chill of autumn nights. (1867)

A large section of the town believe that summer diarrhoea is generated by the insanitary state of the town where it prevails. I dissent entirely from this view. The inhabitants of factory towns...owe their debility to the gradual degeneration of themselves and their forefathers and mothers by factory life until a race is generated which is so debilitated as to be unable to resist the first shock of disease. (1874)

The Collection, Disposal and Utilisation of Town Refuse in Leicester

F.W. Allen, Assistant Borough Surveyor, Leicester, 5 December 1903.

As the town expanded, the first modern network of sewers, laid out in the 1850s, became inadequate. As a stopgap, pail closets were brought in by the Town Council in 1871. Initially, the pails were collected once a week and the night soil was loaded upon railway wagons in a siding on Freak's Ground (now the Rally) and later from Great Northern Railway sidings near Syston Street. Sewage was also loaded onto canal barges from Pasture Lane and St Mary's Wharf. In 1893, 7,000 pails were collected weekly serving an estimated 70,000 to 90,000 people. Despite the Council attempting to fine the contractors for spilling night soil, this nuisance was almost unavoidable.

Owing to these difficulties of sewerage, the pail system was introduced in the year 1871 and many of the water closets and privies were converted into pail closets, the cesspools being filled up and used as ashpits. Pails were provided by the Corporation at a cost of 10s 6d each to the property owner, the Corporation renewing the pails from time to time, as required, without further charge. They also undertook the collection and disposal of the contents. This obtained until the year 1882, after which date no plans were approved shewing anything but water closets.

From this date also open dust-pits and manure-pits were gradually roofed in and ventilated and reduced in dimensions where of large area, and new ones were constructed of very small area, paved at yard level and similarly roofed in and ventilated. Needless to say, the emptying of these confined dust-pits was anything but a healthy occupation, either when very wet (as they frequently were by reason of the throwing in of slops) or when very dry and dusty. Portable dustbins were also provided in isolated cases where the refuse had to be carried through the dwelling house.

In 1886 a sort of unofficial commencement was made in the introduction of a general portable bin system by persuading builders and architects depositing plans to adopt bins in all new property. In many cases the roofed dust-pits were altered and bins provided, the old dust-pit being used as a coal or store place, or sometimes as a bin shed.

Letter to the Sanitary Committee

Inspectors' Office, Leicester, 14 September 1893.
Sir Archdale Palmer was the 52-year-old, Eton-educated 4th Baronet of Wanlip Hall. In September 1893, he decided to find the reason behind the death of large numbers of fish in the River Soar. Using his standing as a magistrate, he inspected various riverside drains and sewers. Although the dead fish were the result of an accidental diversion of sewage into the river from Churchgate, with the aid of the police he uncovered some very dubious practices by the Council's night soil department. The ensuing public debate seems to have sealed the fate of Leicester's pail closet system. He was, without doubt, the author of the anonymous letter referred to below by the police. Mr Freer of the sanitary department was given three months' notice.

Sir,

I beg most respectfully to report of my enquiries of the complaint made in the anonymous letter sent to you by J. Canner Esq., J.P., respecting night soil being emptied from the Corporation boats into the canal and to inform you that at 12.30am on the 14th instant, I, in company with Sergeant Allen, visited the borough yard, Jarvis Street, and found a man named William Lamb, a borough labourer, in a boat (which was laden with street sweepings and pan manure) lying in the canal adjoining the yard. He was bailing the leakage and the liquid which drains from the manure into the bottom of the boat into the canal.

The stench from the liquid was very offensive. Lamb stated that he calculated that there would be about 7 tons of liquid in the boat and he was ordered by Mr Freer, foreman of the sanitary dept., to bail it out into the canal.

I took some of the liquid out of the boat in a bucket and had it brought to the central police station.

I am, Sir, your obedient Servant
James Duns Esq, James Nicholson, Inspector

The Advantages of the Water Closet

Report of the Medical Officer of Health, 1895.

i) Excreted material is removed immediately.
ii) The WC can serve a greater number than the pail closet without causing nuisance, while a pail closet will only contain a certain amount without overflowing, causing the ground around to become filthy and sodden.
iii) Pail closets as a rule are situated in small yards where the airspace is already limited and can ill afford to be polluted by emanations from the pails.
iv) To prevent decomposition the pail contents have to be kept as dry as possible, so urinals have to be erected. A WC with a hinged seat avoids the necessity of separate

The common yard at the back of Nos 28 and 30 St Peter's Lane, in which there were also workshop premises. The primitive looking WC was jointly used by the tenants of Nos 28 and 30. The wall rising above the WC building belonged to No. 2, Court C, St Peter's Lane, in which there were four back-to-back houses.

     urinals.

v)   Emptying pail closets and privies once a week is done away with and the nuisance caused, especially in hot weather, will also disappear and with it the complaints of pail vans and box wagons from people whose night's rest is disturbed by noise and effluvia.

vi)   The difficulty met with in disposing of the collected pail contents is very great, and when a market is obtained the question of transport is found to be an increasing difficulty, as stations are gradually being closed to this kind of manure traffic.

vii)   As regards cost, the water carriage system will be less than the pail system, while the nuisance in collecting and storing at depots will be avoided.

viii)   At the present time there are about 20,000 WCs in Leicester and very few complaints are made about the bad usage of them. The general public are getting more accustomed to using rather than abusing this sanitary convenience.

ix)   Improve the health of the community from sweeter and more cleanly offices attached to their houses.

Pail Closets

Anon, Leicester Oral History Archive, interview 1983.

Our paraffin lamp hung from the ceiling over the scrubbed white table and every morning it would be taken down and the wick trimmed and be refilled with paraffin for the evening. Pail closets were slowly disappearing as piped water was being laid on and taps were taking the place of pumps. Neighbours were proud to use a water closet instead of the old bins that they had been used to. They would stand and wait, just to listen to the flush of the toilet.

Pail Closets

Report of the Medical Officer of Health, 1897.

One pail closet was made to serve two homes and as frequently four houses are found in one yard, two pail closets have been built with a deep ashpit between them. These ashpits are removed at the same time as the pails are converted to WCs. Conversions were started on the triangular section of property lying between Churchgate and Belgrave Gate. Nobody wants to go back to the old system. However, some persons, especially those inhabiting some of the properties let in lodgings, do not appear to have any notion of cleanliness and seem to use the WC in the same filthy way as the pails were formerly used.

'Drug Taking' in the Slums – A Letter from Mrs Bell-Richards

December 1925.
Mrs Mary Bell-Richards was a leader of the Boot and Shoe Trade Union. Her letter came in response to a claim by Cllr Grimsley (a teetotal Methodist preacher) that the habit of women in the slums of drinking methylated spirits mixed with lemon juice was 'enormous'. He said that such drug taking had been proved to be the main cause of bringing 'mentally defective' children into the world. He suggested that 95 per cent of 'feeble minded' children in Leicester came from the slums and that the only way to ensure a mentally and morally sound people was to promote 'sound, clean motherhood'. Mrs Bell-Richards wrote:

For 12 years, as a Guardian of the Poor, I visited every case of childbirth in Wyggeston ward coming under the Poor Law authorities and I never saw or smelt drugs of any kind. I only saw poverty in its vilest form. I write this letter because I am very jealous of the honour of poor women in the slums. I have hundreds of good trade union members out of the 5,000 in the Boot and Shoe Union living in these poor districts. I intend to call a meeting to contest this wholesale charge against poor women in Leicester.

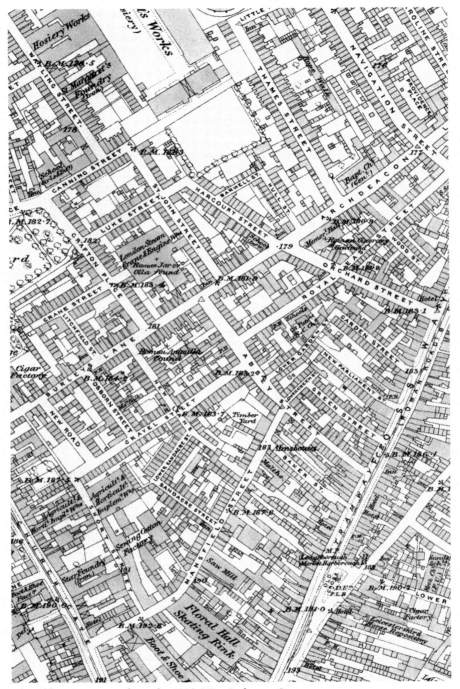

The Abbey Street area from the 1889 25in Ordnance Survey map.

Belgrave Gate from Abbey Street in 1925. Trams had a strangling effect on traffic in Belgrave Gate and, as a result, much of the property on the right of the photograph down as far as the Great Northern Railway Station was demolished so the road could be widened. This work complemented the newly constructed Charles Street bypass.

Abbey Street and Green Street

Tom Barclay, The Wyvern, 28 June 1895.
Joseph Dare wrote in 1851 that: 'our worst localities are in Belgrave Gate and are chiefly inhabited by the Irish and the frequenters of common lodging houses'. The 1851 census records Tom Barclay's father John as a lodger at No. 8 Green Street. That year the Council attempted to force the registration of common lodging houses. It found five common lodging houses in Green Street. The Inspector of Nuisances reported that at No 18: 'in the chamber [bedroom] there were 10 persons sleeping, viz nine men and one woman. In the house-place [living room] there was Martin Lardner and his wife besides a young woman who I found undressed in the pantry. This man has been complained of for taking in lodgers into his house without registering and has been cautioned.'

Has it ever occurred to you, reader, to ask yourself why there should be an Irish colony in many large English towns, and not a Welsh or Scotch one? Here in Leicester the Irish are as nothing compared with such towns as Sheffield, Leeds, Birmingham and Manchester; but their emigration is not to be explained by their exploring tendencies, for they are most conservative in their habits, and removing them from their native soil is like tearing the souls out of them. How then? Well, in 1847 came a failure of the potato crop in Ireland, and it being their principal food they died like rotten sheep and were driven to the four corners of the world. (You must excuse my peculiar figures of speech, for this is an Irish article.) I have often heard them blamed for their seeming inability to get on, for living in slums, for not dressing well, for having no regular trade; but suppose you are an agricultural labourer, overtaken by such a calamity as a famine, and you are forced to flee to a strange country

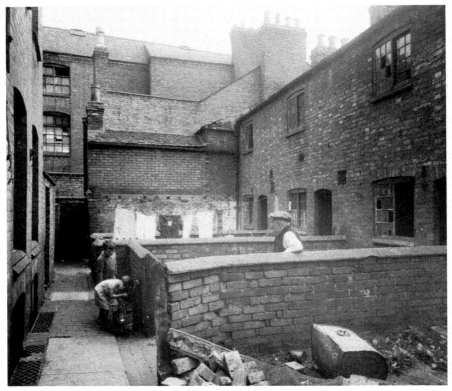

Two children filling bottles with water from the common tap at the rear of Nos 41–47 Abbey Street. These three houses were part of a block on the corner of Royal East Street and Abbey Street and were overshadowed by the two-storey factory building on the left. An open entry to Royal East Street extended along the side of this factory to a gate giving access into the yard of No. 41. The WCs were grouped together just to the left of the top of the entry. The high building in the background is Messrs. John Lee and Son, metal and skin dealers' warehouse. (Author)

where labourers are already plentiful, and the ways of that country are not your ways, and you do not understand its language, and know nothing of its trades and callings. Suppose further that there is a prejudice against you as an intruder, a prejudice against your awkwardness, your religion; and a little unreasoning race hatred, none the better for being pretty mutual, would it not, think you, take all your English pluck and enterprise to surmount all these difficulties?

The Irish settled in Green Street – perhaps attracted by the name – and, of course, the neighbouring streets. They would naturally cling to one another, though often at variance. Contention is better than solitude, says a Celtic proverb, and Celts are not the only people that hate each other for the love of God. Those that could not get navvying and farm work took to 'chip-chopping', 'mat-making' and 'swag'. A swag-basket is a hawker's basket, and is filled with tapes, matches, cotton, laces, buttons, pins and so forth. The more thrifty took larger houses and began to lodge the new arrivals and the 'greeceens'.

The greeceens were the raw recruits that came over every summer to reap the harvest, before the advent of the reaping machine. They had never been out of Erin before and were

Bateman's Row off Sandacre Street was built back-to-back with a large engineering factory. In the background is the windowless rear of the three-storey Bateman's Yard (see overleaf). These houses were probably built in the 1850s by Mr George Bateman, who was originally a painter living in Lower Sandacre Street. By 1861 he was living in Fleckney next door to the vicar and his occupation was given as a 'proprietor of houses'. This row was demolished in 1932 and the tenants rehoused on Martival and Overton Road, paying a rent of 10/6 per week. (Author)

regarded as greenhorns by our anglicised Irish, who regularly chaffed and teased them to the point of a row. Chaff is a great feature of Irish social life as also is the habit of nicknaming. Monkey-mug, Praty-face, Shoulder-the-wind and Shake-the-building are instances of the nickname. Often the greeceen settled down here instead of going back, and soon had a large family – the Irish are as anti-Malthusian as possibly could be. Out of these families of six and seven, brought up somehow in houses of only two small rooms, the eldest and second-eldest sons have enlisted as soon as they were tall and robust enough to carry a musket. There is scarcely an Irish family in the town that has not for the last 30 years furnished one son – generally the eldest – to serve the queen. Many are the bitter curses that have followed her and the colour sergeants from bereaved mothers who would have given 'the two eyes out of their heads' to keep their boys at home. And talking of cursing, the ability of the Irish to curse is something terrible, and shows even in translation, e.g., 'May the hearthstone of hell be their best bed for ever,' and

> 'When your throat fries in hell's drouth,
> Salt the flame be in your mouth,
> For the treachery you did in Aghadoe!' [1]

It is true the correlative terms of endearment are also strong: 'Bright love of my heart, My thousand treasures, A hundred thousand welcomes to you' (*Cead mile failte*). To our sober English minds there is something of an Oriental expression in such phrases. In Green Street itself are no registered lodging houses, but a couple of furnished rooms have been

---

1. From *Aghadoe*, by the Irish poet and playwright John Todhunter (1839–1916).

Bateman's Yard (Court A, Sandacre Street). This was the rear of three houses that faced on to Sandacre Street. The houses were demolished in 1932. Note the wooden buttress on the right holding the wall in place.

let to people who must live somewhere, and who, though belonging to the weaker sex, are no worse than the stronger sex which supports them in their strange calling and meanwhile escapes blame. But inspectors know more about these things than I, and they have been turning certain lodging houses in Abbey Street upside down.

In Lower Green Street, which joins Green Street at right angles, a couple of houses are to let, owing to a late family quarrel that resulted in a broken arm to one of the quietest women in the world. The chief aggressor was a woman too (save the mark). There are in the neighbourhood about here some late arrivals from goodness knows where and they are awful people for drinking and rowing. The quieter neighbours are heartily sick of them. Most Irish have such an excess of energy that, apparently, they must fight now and then. In the old faction fights, one of the greatest difficulties was to find an excuse for a shindy when there was no natural one. Men fought for the pure love of the thing. In one of Banim's delightful tales we have a picture of a celebrated character who was always notified of impending fights, for he was very handy with the kipeen, and a match for any three men. Each side would try to enlist his services, but though he promised each he waited till he saw how the fortunes of war went, then he would be sure to throw himself on the side of the weaker party. All this is changed both in Ireland and England. The Green Street fights are past; more than half the inhabitants of the street are English, and the rest, the Irish, are (allow me the bull) quite English, you know.

We have not a word of the old language of the mother country, and divil a taste of the brogue remains with us either. I am talking of the present generation: the old stagers are going all over to the majority. They live to a patriarchal age. It will be half a century next year since some of them came out of their own land, and they have seen many hardships;

Bailey's Yard, Sandacre Street, c.1930. The 21 houses adjoining this yard had to share one tap and an outside gully. The common WCs are in the foreground on the right, while further back there is a three-storey factory (shown as a leather laces factory on a 1931 map). These houses were back-to-back with houses facing on to Lower Sandacre Street. The tenants were rehoused on Martival and Overton Road. (Author)

but they are alive: deaf and doddering and croffling, but alive. Here is an old chap sitting today out in the sun; he is veritably in his second childhood, and it is pretty to see the children, active as goats, though not barefooted as they would have been 30 years ago, playing round his knees – first childhood and second childhood together. His granddaughter has to wash and scrub him as she would a child and he complains like a child; but there's only a handful of him and he has to submit. His companions are nearly gone, or bide in the workhouse that was unknown to them 'at home in the ould counthry'. Their sons and grandsons know nought and care nought for the history and language of their race. Many of them have dropped the O's and Mac's of their names in deference to English feeling; Crochans have become Crowsons, Munroes Rowes, Faheys Fays. The brogue that once you could have cut with a knife, so thick was it, is extinct; and not a soul knows the difference between *The Boyne Water* and *The Wearing of the Green*. The wake is gone for ever, though small regret have I for that; but *O Wirras' thrua!* the absence of the flute-player, and the shaking of the foot to *Apples in Winter, Miss McLeod's Reel, The Connacht Man's Ramble* and *Haste to the Wedding*.

In Green Street rents are rather high and improvements rather low, if not absent altogether. In the back lanes [Lower Garden Street] that opens out of Abbey Street, some property has been condemned. To show the fondness of the Irish for the same spot, I may mention that one man has lived in Green Street 40 years and before the building of the present house lived in a previous one on the same spot.

I went into Abbey Street, where, leaving out the slaughterhouses, marine stores and bakeries, the remainder are public houses and lodging houses. Enter we a lodging house

A lodging house at Nos 22 and 20 Abbey Street. No. 22 is next to a junction with Mansfield Street. This may well be the house Barclay mentions previously. On demolition, 19 people were displaced from No. 20 but they were not rehoused by the Corporation. These houses were demolished in 1932. (Author)

Court C, Abbey Street, Cock Muck Hill Almshouses, c.1930. These buildings were used for six poor persons chosen by the parish officers and who were not receiving relief. The almshouses had been built in 1782, when original houses on Cock Muck Hill were pulled down as a result of a previous widening of Belgrave Gate. They were rebuilt in Abbey Street around an open court. Sometime before 1782 Catherine Holmes left money to provide the inhabitants with coal on St Thomas's Day. (Author)

kept by a quiet widow, who will not have the drunkard and the rowdy inside her door if she knows it. The rooms are plentifully furnished with drawers and crockery; on one wall is a picture of the Crucifixion, on another the ascension of Mary into heaven. Rosary beads hang over the mantelpiece, and St Patrick, mitred and crosier in hand, banishes the snakes. Fascinating Irish girls march up and down outside with nothing on their heads, and everybody sits outside the door these evenings. They are extreme, these Irish; rather ugly or very good looking; very quiet or perfect 'devil's limbs'. The ugliness is all with the mature males. I call in at the Old Cheese, where most they congregate, and then at the George the Third, where the counterfeit presentments of famous prizefighters, to the number of 30, do grace the walls. Here are Tug Wilson, Prussian, Peter Jackson, J.L. Sullivan, Jem Corbett, Charley Mitchell, Paddy Ryan, Kilrain, Dempsy, Macauliffe and many more. I went up higher towards Belgrave Gate and had a look at the slab that tells the why and the wherefore of the almshouses in the Cock Muck Hill yard, founded 1782 and managed by the guardians of the parish of St Margaret. These are small two-roomed huts. I miss the old calaighs in plain shoulder-shawls and bordered caps, who used in these parts, years ago, to squat on their hunkers and smoke dudheens.[2]

An impulsive, reckless, light-hearted, easy-going race are 'the Oirish', as our English friends call them; certainly not without their faults, but – 'I met a hundred men on the road to Delhi, and they were all my brothers' – as the Hindu proverb says; and that means, I suppose, that we all have our faults, of whatever nationality we are.

---

2. A short tobacco pipe.

Nos 1–4 Gravel Street and Short Street. This shows the junction and a Leicester Co-operative Printers' lorry being repaired. The building next to the factory entrance on Short Street was a back-to-back house which faced out onto a courtyard. This courtyard led to the back of houses on Churchgate and there was a similar courtyard further up Short Street. These houses were demolished in 1932. There were two Short Streets in Leicester, the other being renamed West Short Street to reduce confusion. (Author)

Children playing in a yard at the rear of Sandacre Street, c.1930. (Author)

Above: Looking up Burley's Lane, which continues in the distance as Archdeacon Lane. The junction with Abbey Street is on the right.

Below: The heart of Leicester's Irish quarter: a view of Green Street looking towards Lower Green Street.

Above: Court D, Mansfield Street looking from the entry in Mansfield Street. The photograph shows a row of rear wall blank cottages which backed on to a timberyard. The entry by the lamp led to the court shown on the left.

Washing being done in a corner of Court D off Mansfield Street. Many of the houses in this area had no internal water supply or sink. Overshadowing these houses was the beer bottling plant on the corner of Abbey and Mansfield Street. These houses were slightly closer to Gravel Street than Mansfield Street and were tucked away behind Nos 107 and 108 Gravel Street. They were demolished in 1932 and the tenants were rehoused on Martival and Overton Road. (Author)

Looking down Sandacre Street from Mansfield Street towards Lower Sandacre Street. The workman's hut is next to the site of a demolished pub on the corner of Mansfield Street. At the end of the street can be seen the three-storey buildings of Bateman's Yard and the entrance to Bateman's Row. St Margaret's Church is just visible in the background and the entrance to Bailey's Yard is on the right before the turn. These houses were demolished in 1932 and the tenants rehoused on Overton Road and Martival, paying a rent of 10/6. Their old rent was 6/- to 8/-. (Author)

Report of the Medical Officer of Health on the Abbey Street Area

February 1929.
In 1929, the Medical Officer of Health presented a report on the houses in the area surrounding what is now St Margaret's bus station (Abbey Street, Green Street, Sandacre Street, Mansfield Street, Garden Street, Gravel Street and New Road.) Here the infant mortality rate was nearly double the city average, while the incidence of TB, smallpox and scarlet fever was also much higher. Although this was viewed as Leicester's worst area of slum housing, its dilapidation and lack of adequate sanitary provision was not unique. The Medical Officer of Health recommended that the most satisfactory way of dealing with 'the evils' connected with such houses, courts and alleys was to rearrange and reconstruct the streets and houses.

The general layout of the area is distinctly bad as every available piece of land in the area had been utilised for building purposes. There are 243 buildings on approximately 3.39 acres, which gives an average of 71.6 per acre as compared with 7.42 for the whole city.
Drainage: Many downspouts were found to be directly connected to the drains, thus acting as ventilators to the sewers and allowing foul gases access to the houses below

The rear of Nos 1–15 New Parliament Street, taken from No. 17 and looking towards Lower Garden Street and Royal East Street. Today the rear of the St James Hotel and multi-storey car park would completely obscure this view.

Lower Sandacre Street, looking from the turn of Sandacre Street towards New Lane. The houses on the right-hand side were back-to-back houses with those on Bailey's Yard. The entry to the yard was situated about halfway down. (Author)

the roofs. In one instance 21 houses have the use of one gully in the yard. There is inadequate drainage and this, combined with the lack of proper provision for supplying water, is not conducive to that state of cleanliness which is required.

Sinks: 11 per cent are of a glazed type with a tap above, and 78 per cent are not provided with sinks

WCs: 10 houses are supplied with a separate WC and in the worst instance six WCs were shared by 20 houses.

Water Supply: 32 houses have taps over sinks. The remainder have to obtain water from taps in the yards used in common with other houses. In many cases the number of taps is not sufficient.

Clothes washing: The larger proportion of the houses are entirely without any means for the proper washing of clothes. In some instances, where washing coppers are provided, water taps and proper drainage facilities are absent.

Food stores: Ill-lighted and ill-ventilated cupboards in living rooms adjoining chimney breasts. The tenants complain of the futility of trying to keep food fresh for more than a short time.

The free circulation of air around the houses is prevented by the cramped nature of the buildings, while the lack of dustbins means that the meagre yards were often scattered with decaying rubbish. The population density of 283 people per acre is 10 times the average for the whole city. Factories overshadow the houses to such an extent that artificial light had to be used in daytime to enable the survey to take place. 40 per cent of the houses have only two rooms and 28 per cent were either back-to-back houses or of a rear wall blank type (without a rear exit and windows).

The rear of No. 1 Court A, Garden Street (off Belgrave Gate). Could the furniture in the yard be awaiting removal to a new Council house?

Above: A view down Mansfield Street towards Abbey Street and Lower Green Street. The parked car is opposite the top of Sandacre Street and the site of a demolished pub. The wooden building seen on the right was a saw mill. Behind the three-storey houses on the right (Nos 48–45) was a courtyard of five cottages. (Author)

Below: The rear of Nos 53–59 Mansfield Street awaiting demolition in 1932. Lavatories can be seen on the extreme left with a tap in the middle of the common yard. These houses were adjacent to W. Tomkins boot and shoe factory. (Author)

The rear of Nos 107–108 Gravel Street c.1930 next to Pollard's bottling plant, which was on the corner of Abbey Street. Mrs Powell is one of the ladies in the photograph. (Author)

New Road in the summer of 1937. The view shows Nos 6, 8, 10 and 12 looking from Burley's Lane towards Gravel Street. The hoardings at the end of the street are where Nos 3–11 Gravel Street once stood. The 40ft high Co-op Printing Works on the right-hand side completely overshadows Nos 14–20 at the end of the street. These houses were demolished in 1937 and the tenants rehoused on Hand Avenue and Raven Road. (Author)

Growing Up in New Road

George Stacey, Leicester Oral History Archive, 1983.

The houses in New Road were dark, small, dingy, damp and, in some cases, rat infested. I remember well one particular house, next door to where we lived, which consisted of two rooms: one room downstairs and one room upstairs. In that particular family there were seven people. That meant mother and father and five children, three boys and two girls, and they slept with a blanket hung between the beds to make the division.

Over the weekend Mother would make a parcel up of bedding and clothes of some sort and on Monday morning would go along to Harry Freestones the pawnshop in Sanvey Gate and perhaps get half a crown for the parcel of clothes. I can not remember whether it was a fortnight or a month you had to redeem it, but in that time, somehow someway, she would scrape together the half a crown plus the interest. I would go along there, pay the money over and bring back the clothes. Dad's suit would also go down there.

The Bedford Street area of Leicester. This map is a composite of two OS maps from the 1880s.

'The Cross' or junction of Belgrave Gate (left) with Bedford Street (right) before the building of Charles Street in 1931. This was an important junction since Belgrave Gate was the road north and Bedford Street led into the populous Wharf Street area.

Bedford Street

Tom Barclay, The Wyvern, 31 May 1895.

I suppose most Leicester people, gentle and simple, know the latitude and longitude of Bedford Street, alias 'Barkby Lane'. It is a thin, narrow-gutted streak of a street – a working-man's street between the aristocratic Belgrave Gate and the bourgeois Wharf Street. It [Bedford Street] empties itself into Russell Square at one end and 'The Cross' at the other where it becomes confluent with Belgrave Gate. There are in it more second-hand clothes shops to the square yard than in any other street in Leicester. Old brokers' shops are also strongly in evidence, but they do not jostle one another like the old clothes shops. Second-hand shoe shops do also greatly abound. One gets wondering who patronises these emporiums of left-off clobber; but consider the tramps, travellers, hawkers, pensioners and boozers, and perhaps a few poachers. Look at these sunburnt, shuffling haggard-featured men grouped outside the lodging houses to sniff the evening breeze in this sultry weather; these ravaged, wasted women, contorted, made angular, beaten and battered out of all beauty of form by the privations of good food and clothes, and the hardships of the road. These, and the boozers, who would think it a horrible waste of good money to purchase new clothes, must be clad somehow: so hither they repair alone with inmates of the 'terraces' of Palmerstone Street and the denizens of that 'pack-man's puzzle', Martin Street.

Probably half of Leicester comes to this street for left-offs. You see we can get a complete rig-out, from garret to basement, from 'tile' to 'Lord Mayors' inclusive, for about 10/-. Eh? You do not know what Lord Mayors are? Why, second-hand boots 'shomocks'

Above: A court at the rear of No. 105 Belgrave Gate, which was opposite Green Street and New Parliament Street. It was demolished in 1937 and became the site of Kingstones department store.

The drinking fountain dated January 1869 at the junction of Bedford Street and Belgrave Gate. In 1960, the fountain was offered to Leicester Museum, who declined to take it. It was consequently broken up.

The entrance to Court J at the rear of Nos 139–143 Belgrave Gate, which was just opposite Orchard Street. This court backed on to the houses in Wilton Street.

– and they resemble the people that buy them in that they are wrinkled and crinkled, flabby and shrunken, patched up and 'about done up'. We can get a good pair for about 'eighteen win', which is why we poor people get corns and riding toes and have to drag our legs from the knee downwards.

We have got eight or nine pubs, and some of them sell the vilest of vile beer; but I would not say which for the world. Besides, it is not the fault of the landlords the houses are tied. Strange that we should apply that term 'landlord' to publicans who often have not as much land as would go in a flowerpot! I say eight or nine pubs, but practically we have about 12 or 13, for the back ways of the Chariot, the Diadem and Hassock, the Goose, and the Dragon, open into our street from Belgrave Gate.

The courts and passages are, I suppose, much of a muchness with all the courts and passages that have been, are now and ever will be. In Paradise Row, which saving your presence suggests the other place more than Paradise, there is a two-roomed house to let for 2/6. In this row there are three or four miserable pretences of gardens, each about a yard and a half square surrounded by closets no bigger than rabbit-hutches. Faugh! the poor squalid inhabitants! The whole place, people and surroundings are most depressing. Mind you, we are not all in courts and lodging houses. There is the variety of pork pie manufactory, a bobbin factory and a couple of marine stores. Then we have a couple of 'model' lodging houses, one of them called 'The Workman's Home'. Other public buildings are the Labour Club and the Ragged School Mission, and a large shoe factory. Opposite the latter we have a row of houses and two of them, 98 and 100, are shut up because they harboured 'unfortunates'. We do not know what has become of the unfortunates – whether they have been killed, converted or have only migrated. Up higher towards Belgrave Gate are more courts; and sometimes in one and the same court we have

The Griffin Inn, next to the hoarding, had an entrance on Bedford Street (above) and on Belgrave Gate (left). In 1851, the landlord Mr Robert Woodhouse was reprimanded by the Council for the nuisance caused by his pigs. The building was replaced in 1929 and the pub later became Jacey's Bar.

a three-roomed house rented at 3/3 and a 'ready furnished' one rented at 5/3. And some of the aforesaid 'unfortunates', whose calling would appear to be almost irrepressible, though held to be so nefarious, manage to become tenants of the 'ready furnished' till a drunken shindy ousts them.

Of fried-fish shops we have a couple and the purveyors of eatables for our lodging house population are fearfully and wonderfully supplied. Not only do we wear left-offs, drink adulterated beer and dream away the happy hours in a 'fourpenny doss', but we eat the poorest and worst grub into the bargain. Just gaze into this shop as a specimen. Here are the things that are bought, aye, and eaten with a relish! What a set-out! 'Gristles' made of goodness knows what, the surface of it baked into a rind by the sun, until resembling a dirty slab of plum pudding; chitterlings, commonly called 'chitlins'; pickles; 'scratchings'; hog's pudding; unhealthy-looking bacon; greasy 'chawl'; and dried-up, stale-looking 'faggots', each with 'a varicose vein on the top' as I lately heard an imaginative anarchist lecturer describe it. These be some of my impressions of Bedford Street in this year of our Lord; pray you and your readers like them. But an ye like them or not, there they be without exaggeration as I think, and certainly not set down in malice.

Above: The rear of Nos 2–26 Lower Grove Street looking towards the Methodist Church on Belgrave Gate, close to today's flyover. The church later became the Co-op Hall and then the Leicester Square. This common yard had three water closets and was shared by eight houses. The rent for these houses in the 1930s was between 4/5 and 7/-. The buildings on Belgrave Gate were demolished c.1930 for a road widening scheme. This photograph was taken from the back bedroom window of No. 19 Grovesnor Street. Below: The rear of Nos 183–193 Belgrave Gate in September 1930. This picture was taken from No. 14 Lower Grove Street (shown above) before the road widening scheme.

Residents of Britannia Street in the 1930s. The lack of a dustbin for every house was a frequent cause of rubbish being scattered around courtyards. (Author)

Britannia Street

Tom Barclay, The Wyvern, *5 July 1895.*

I have spoken of the lodging houses of Bedford Street and Abbey Street, but they hide their diminished heads before those of Britannia Street, with the illuminated lamps and large gable-end written advertisements. The Victoria Model lodging house is a large, new, solidly built place, with all the appearances of a working men's club. Outside, between the first and second stones, are bas-relief figures in terracotta of the four British nationalities: English, Irish, Scotch and Welsh. Passing through the corridors, you are aware of left and right wings to the building, consisting of enamelled brick-lined lavatories. If you want a private cupboard for your 'tommy', you can be accommodated; you pay 6d for the key to one and when you leave the establishment the 6d is returned to you. But if you choose to leave your food about, quite accessible to your mates, they never touch it. The reception room and refectory are one and the same room and the walls are covered with a most entertaining series of pictures – Daniel Lambert, Lord Salisbury, prizefighters and Derby winners.

The framed rules announce that no intoxicating drink is allowed upon the premises nor

Left: The Victoria Model lodging house, Britannia Street, 1887. Its architect was Thomas Hind, who also designed the Co-op store on the High Street. Hind was a Liberal Town Councillor and active member of the Leicester Co-operative Society. Right: The junction of Wilton Street and Belgrave Gate in the autumn of 1929. (The Leicester Mercury)

smoking upstairs. No washing will be undertaken on Saturdays or Sundays. No gambling is permitted and no admission given after 11pm. About 7pm saunter in the hawkers and drovers, and the shuffling of the heavy-shod feet of navvies is heard. Food is produced from pockets – eggs, bacon, beef, mutton chops – and frying pans are set hissing. In several cases the meal is already prepared, awaiting the hungry. Every man knows his own teapot by some little private mark; caddies and basins are produced. Still they come, sturdy fellows with arm-muscles like a Hercules pull off their pilot jackets with the great ivory buttons, muffler and flat cap and wash before sitting at the board. What would some of your readers give for their digestions.

'A peasant's sweat is worth his lord's estate', says Byron.

The conversation is of work. 'Did you have any chance up there?', 'I made a start today at...', 'I shall have to be off tomorrow to...' The men are rather weary. The deputy comes round to put the crockery in its proper place. He asks if anyone wants a check for a bed. The prices of beds are from 4d to 8d. The establishment finds all crockery and cooking utensils, but lodgers board themselves. The cooking range would not shame a Stoneygate mansion. No women are allowed at this house: the place for them is further up the street. Harry Wilkinson, the proprietor, is also the owner of the property and superintends things himself. He has two other models and several small houses in the same street. His memory is great, his word is law; he never gets excited; he is generally respected. If he tells an applicant that he can not be admitted that applicant goes away quietly.

Other lodging houses are a repetition of this, with a sprinkling of the tramp order thrown in – that order with the straw-coloured hair and the pinched, hungry, haggard, sunburnt features; a 'stook o'duds' on its poor slouching, angular back and with all its goods and chattels tied in a kerchief; worn down by continuous and excessive travel, and ever travelling in the worst possible foot-gear.

Russell Square in the early 1950s. The junction with Britannia Street was next to the Andrewes Foundry. (Newarke Houses Museum)

Has drink anything to do with this order specially? I think not. Drink affects all classes of workers about equally. Its temples have their foundations deep in our society. The well-to-do drink because they can afford it; the ordinary worker for sociability and to vary the monotony of doing the same thing thousands of times in a week; the unemployed and the wastrel take it as a drug. Some are made morose and pugnacious by it, some drowsy and stupid; some hilarious and generous, some maudlin and sentimental. Let us enter a specimen of one of its temples. The great polished brass bar in front of the counter is convenient to lean on and prevents the drinker's coat-sleeve becoming drink-soaked. Then there is a footrest at the bottom of the counter and sawdust in a trough to be expectorated into. Everything round gleams bewilderingly. The hot water urns are electroplated, so are the handles of the beer machines. A couple of brass statuettes of Punch are fastened to the counter, with small cigar-shaped brass jets issuing from their mouths: these are to light your pipe or cigar. Spills are cut ready in a tumbler. The cigar box itself, made of mahogany, stands on the mahogany sideboard, amid a display of crystal in several colours, that is all doubled by a large mirror let into the wall immediately at the back. On this sideboard are tankards, carafes, decanters, and glass barrels of dark red port and amber-coloured whiskey, with small porcelain buckets suspended from their taps to catch the precious droppings. Cornices, panels, shelves and brackets are gilded or painted in bright, positive colours. *Tivoli*, *Empire* and other bills hang beside the counter, and a file of the *Leicester Sporting News*. An attractive girl stands behind serving, and the swish of liquids rushing through pipes is heard amid the rinsing and clinking of glasses and the hum and buzz and chatter and laughter of 50 persons of both sexes and all ages, from 16 to 60.

This spacious building, with all its pomp and glitter, is not 20 yards from dirty, dismal, disordered homes. These are all sorts and ages in Britannia Street, the new buildings looking some places more blank and forbidding than the old houses. The courts are again

The children of Alfred Terrace in 1934. There were about 40 houses on Alfred Terrace, which was a cul-de-sac off Alfred Street, midway between Bedford Street and Wharf Street.

numerous, and they come between the Melton Street back gardens and the Woodboy Street back gardens. But the [most] dismal, [most] squalid, worst hovels I have yet seen are in Woodboy Yard (as it used to be called), which goes through from Britannia Street to Woodboy Street. These are close to Belgrave Gate; the doors are not set up straight and a tall man would have to stoop to enter them. The cupboards look like a bit of board let into a hole. The walls are damp, and the yard, being narrow, is miserably dark. In short there is neither room nor light, and whether there was cleanliness I could not well see. Mr Wilkinson's 'Models' are indeed palaces compared with these holes. For myself, I could not feel comfortable in one of them an hour; their very contact makes me shudder. I sincerely pity their poor occupants and cannot help wondering whether they can keep themselves healthy.

I remember Britannia Street while Melton Street, Junction Road, and the whole of the streets between it and Belgrave, still were not [built]. It was the outside street of the town on its own side of Belgrave Gate. Its boatmen inhabitants were once a bit of a terror, but canal traffic has declined in favour of the railway and

'The boatmen oh,
Sailing down the river hi-ho,'

has disappeared. There is no pub in the street, the license of a house that is now the Star lodging house having been taken away years ago; but the Britannia is at one end and the Full Moon at the other, and the Durham Ox, British Lion and Sultan come fast and furious. The latter pub, having been pulled down to make room for St Mark's Church, simply went and stood across the street. To these shrines come all the thirsty pilgrims of Foundry and Russell Squares, and of Crab Street, Woodboy Street and Britannia Street.[1]

---

1. The unfortunately named Crab Street has since become the pious St Mark's Street.

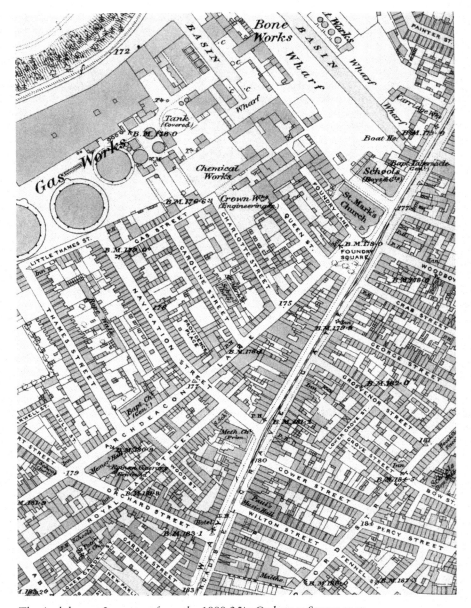

The Archdeacon Lane area from the 1889 25in Ordnance Survey map.

A common yard at the rear of Burley's Lane where Tom Barclay spent some of his early years. (Author)

Memoirs And Medleys: The Autobiography of A Bottle Washer

Tom Barclay, 1924, an excerpt from his autobiography published in 1934.

What a monotonous childhood! No toys, no picture books, no pets, no going 'ta-ta'. No carpet on the uneven brick floor, no mat, no wallpaper; what poverty! There was neither doctor nor midwife present at my birth, of that I am convinced. Indeed, I have heard Mother boast that she never needed a midwife. She was very hardy, brought up in the wilds of the 'county Mayo, God help us!' After all, why should a woman not be able to bring forth like cats and cows and other mammals?

Here in this 18ft-square court off Burley's Lane, Leicester, St Margaret's bells rang dismally every Sunday morning as I tried to play with duck-stones for toys. I am afraid the one door and one chamber window of the two-roomed crib we lived in were seldom opened, though not 6ft from the muck hole and the unflushed privies, and air could only get in from one side of the house. How did we remain healthy? But let me not imagine that because others were born in country cottages and manses with meads that slope away in front and windswept hills in view that therefore they lived happy ever after. Open-air exercises, a sumptuous table, purple and fine linen and a university education awaiting, yes: but in spite of all these, they will suffer disappointments, boredom, weariness, perhaps poverty, and some will murder or be murdered, while poverty-stricken *moi qui parle* may end up calm as a Buddha and in tune with the Infinite.

After the monotony and dreariness of that Burley's Lane hut, I somehow find myself in a similar two-roomed hut in a similar court in a similar slum – Abbey Street: our walls

71

Court A, Charter Street (previously Charlotte Street). This view shows the backs of Nos 9–13 Caroline Street, complete with fractured and perished brickwork. On the right was one of two back-to-back houses in the court. Two water taps and three WCs were shared by the nine households. Joseph Langton (born c.1860), a retired shoe rivetter, is the elderly man in the centre of the picture. He had been living in Charter Street since the turn of the century. The tenants were rehoused on Hand Avenue in 1937. (Author)

are now plastered with wood-cuts from newspapers, and there are mounds of thick ice all round the gutters. Now there are five of us sleeping in one little upper room. I remember nothing of this locale but the attitudinising of kiddies in the yard doubling their fists and prattling of the great fight between Sayers and Heenan.[1] We were commanded to remain shut in, Father and Mother being out most of the day earning a living. Father knew no trade and to dig [he] was not able: he collected rags and bones, rag-bag on back, without as much as a truck (or handcart). Mother worked at a rag-shop or marine store dealer's, or she got blocks of wood from the woodyards, chopped them small and sold the chips in pen'norths for fire-lighting round the neighbouring streets.[2]

'Now see that ye don't stir a foot out of this till me or yer mother comes back, or I'll tan the life out of ye, do ye hear?' Such the command, but it was not in juvenile flesh and blood to obey always.

The scene changes once more, and we are again still in a two-roomed pigsty-crib in a court off Woodboy Street, but all dreariness is gone, exchanged for alarms and excursions, chases and flights and mad uproar. How could anyone resist breaking out of that dirty

---

1. Sayers was the first English boxer to fight an international match when he fought American John C. Heenan at Farnborough, Hampshire, on 17 April 1860.
2. Marine store dealers were those who dealt in anything that was supposed to exist on board a ship, including bones, rags and old bottles.

Above: The rear of Nos 9–19 Navigation Street taken from Providence Place. This yard was used by 15 three-storey houses, all of which had a back living room, an extra bedroom and a pantry for food storage added at the rear. This necessitated the building of tall chimneys. (Author) Below: Providence Place looking towards Gas Street. The houses with no rear doors or windows are the rear of Court B, which was reached via an entry from Navigation Street. The rear of 23–27 Navigation Street are on the left. The cottages on the right backed onto a court behind Caroline Street (see overleaf). This land later became the forecourt of J.W. Kempton's hosiery factory on Archdeacon Lane.

A courtyard which was situated next to Providence Place and between Caroline Street and Navigation Street.

kennel on a summer's day when the sun shone even into that court. We broke bounds and ran up and down the street like little mad things.

Why had we to stay in? Well, you see, we might get lost or run over or beaten, hounded and ill-used by the Sassenach kids: as a matter of fact we were hounded and harassed.

'Hurroo Mick! Ye Awrish Paddywack. Arrah, bad luck to the ships that brought ye over!'

These were the salutes from the happy English child: we were battered, threatened, elbowed, pressed back to the door of our kennel amid boos and jeers and showers of small missiles. The unkind expressions must have been borrowed from the grown-ups, whose animosity was often evident enough. To tell the truth, Sassenach kids fought among themselves; street fought street and district fought district without the slightest cause. And after all, why expect youths (who are mentally but at the Stone Age period) not to fight without cause while grown-ups, backed and abetted by college professors and ministers of Jesus Christ, fight with almost as little? I would like to know, and I wish I were anthropologist and psychologist enough to answer, is there any such reality as race-

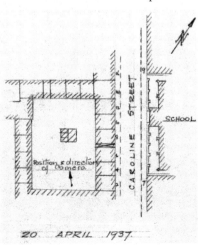

The location of the above photograph. Many of the pictures taken by the Council's Health Department in the 1930s had maps carefully drawn in pencil on the reverse.

74

Above: The rear of Nos 20–30 Navigation Street, looking from Archdeacon Lane towards the gasworks, the canal and Abbey Park. Navigation Street went from Belgrave Gate, by the current flyover, down towards the gasworks and canal. A health inspector can be seen holding a measure on the lower right of the picture. The row of seven houses on the left, Cope's Cottages, did not face on to a road, but instead were reached via an entry between the houses on Navigation Street on the right. Behind these cottages was another yard at the rear of Thames Street. In the 19th century this had housed a rope walk and sties containing 14 pigs.
Below: Chickens peck for scraps round the dustbins and toilet in a yard in Gas Street. (Author)

Children playing among dustbins in the yard adjacent to Nos 4 and 5 Court B, Caroline Street. The cottages on the right are Nos 1–4 Court A, while the cottages in the background were situated in Berridges's Yard, Navigation Street. Note the washing boiler with a drainpipe chimney. The tenants were rehoused in 1937 on Cort Crescent and Didsbury Avenue and the houses demolished in 1940. (Author)

hatred? There should not be among intelligent grown-up people. My own attitude towards a foreigner of whatever colour or creed is simply one of interest [and] intense curiosity. And this makes me social: the only thing that might repel me, or make me cold, is denseness, want of mentality; but this repels me in men of my own nationality.

But what filthy little wretches we children were, and how could it be otherwise? Not Papuans nor Basutos nor Fijians could I think be more degraded. And this was in the middle of the 19th century. O great and glorious empire! What chance to be clean was there in a house on whose only floor bags of dusty rags and putrescent bones were spilled out to be sorted? Nevertheless, we were used to this, and before going to bed we all knelt down on the bare uneven brick floor and recited the Rosary, father leading off: one Our Father to 10 Hail Mary's: one of the prayers spoken 50 times by the help of a string of beads and we arose feeling good and comforted and strengthened for the morrow's work. We used to say very devoutly 'Forgive us our trespasses as we forgive them that trespass against us,' and we used to forget that we very seldom did forgive.

One day the kids from the other end of the court or 'yard', as we called it, attacked us under Billy their leader, and broke a pane of glass and thrust a rod through. Unable to get out, or fearful of a spanking if we did, we scuttled upstairs and threw cinders from the chamber window on Billy and his pals; they battered the door and we retaliated as we could. My imagination went to work: Billy was King William and we were the Irish: it was the siege of Limerick being in some mysterious manner enacted over again. There it was, Gael and Sassenach once more. What neighbours' quarrels

The rear of Court B, Caroline Street. The Belgrave Gate gasworks can be seen in the background with gasometer and overhead transporter. This yard was common to 14 houses, with one water tap and five WCs for the joint use of all the tenants. Nos 1, 2 and 3 Court B (in the foreground) had 4½in brickwork which was badly bulged and fractured. Nos 4 and 5 just show on the far side of the yard (see opposite). The boundary wall of the yard in the background was also the back of four rear wall blank-type houses in Court A. Nine houses (Nos 20–36) which fronted on to Caroline Street also backed onto this court. The tenants were rehoused in 1937 on Hand Avenue and the houses demolished in 1940. (Author)

when father and mother came back, what fine excuses for our conduct, why should we not defend ourselves? There followed weltings and wailings, but I can not blame father and mother for venting their anger: the whole crib from floor to roof showed but too horribly a state of siege.

What sort of an existence was it where a mother giving suck had to be hours away from home trying to earn something? When the kids of the yard were not molesting us, I as eldest was nurse, and often have I put my tongue into baby's mouth to be sucked in lieu of 'titty' to stop her cries. The cries used to cease for a minute and then were resumed as the tongue gave no satisfaction. Poor, cooped-up, vermin-infested brats! But I am suffering much more now probably in simply remembering our state than I actually suffered then: we did not feel the dimness and squalor and foul smells, the horror of the bugs and lice and black beetles as I now, many years after feel them: we had no other life, no other sensations and feelings. This was life, and we knew no other to contrast it with. Does the worm wish to be a butterfly, or the mole a lark?

What is 'chin cough' and how should it be cured? I suspect chin cough was whooping cough: Mother's cure for it was a drink out of the chalice. I and my brother were taken to the chapel and, kneeling before the altar-rails, the kind priest gave us a drink out of

Nos 37–39 Caroline Street and No. 21 Gas Street in the late 1930s. The photograph shows the Belgrave Gate gasworks, the overhead transporter and the lower end of Caroline Street where it joined with Gas Street, near to the gasworks entrance. The house on the corner with the lean-to scullery was No. 21 Gas Street, and the two houses adjoining were Nos 37 and 39 Caroline Street. Nos 32–39 Caroline Street and No. 21 Gas Street were sold by auction in January 1935 for £875, or £146 for each house. (Author)

the sacramental chalice: I do not know whether the liquor was wine or water, or whether it cured us.

There is a proverb that the grey mare is often the best horse. Mother was the grey mare of our family: untiring energy, unfailing health, hope and faith, and never a new dress, never a holiday, never any leisure or amusement, never I fear even a generous meal of victuals. All work and no play, but still not dull. I am sure we never had a complete bath in all our childhood years, unless such a thing is indispensable to the newly born. Mother did all that was possible, but she had neither time nor means to boil our rags of shirts and sheets when washing. We had no wash tub nor dolly pegs, not to speak of wringing and mangling machines: there could have been no room for such in a room only 9ft by 9ft, even had we possessed them, eh, Mother? So we went unwashed, and pediculosis thrived greatly in his two principal species, *capitis* and *vestimenti*, and God's beautiful image was prayed upon daily and nightly. No fault of Mother's.

She was not permitted, even had she the money and leisure, to indulge in beer and dominoes of an evening like my father; her consolation was an old Irish lamentation or love song and the contemplation of the sufferings of 'Our Blessed Lord' and his virgin mother. We males can revert to paganism and forget for an hour or two in revel and song the Man of Sorrows, the poor gibbetted God: where now, while we are carousing, are Gethsemane and Calvary? We are lapped in the Elysium of ale and skittles and cards. We are no Christians tonight, but Bacchanals. The woman, the mother is at the same time and

Court D, Archdeacon Lane, where six houses shared three WCs and a washing copper. The entrance to this court was a 10ft-wide passage between Nos 82 and 84 Archdeacon Lane, which is to the left of the woman with the pram. The court lay between Charter Street and Queen Mary Street. At the bottom of the yard (not shown) were Nos 3 and 5, which were back-to-back. (Author)

hour kneeling at the feet of the Blessed Virgin, or scheming and troubling how she shall pay next week's shop and rent. We get credit till Saturday from the little grocer's shop at the corner, but we must pay each Saturday or have to go hungry all next week...

As with the previous dens, our door in the court in Woodboy Street was seldom open in summer and hardly ever in winter: it would never do to let the cold in. I suppose such exist even to this day. Two little rooms, one up and one down, and air, the air of a court too, having entrance and exit by one side of the house only. I say 'to this day' and this is the year of 1924, of Wembley wonders and Empire pageants. Poor as we were, we were not the poorest in the court; the very poorest were too proud to let the others know how poor they were: they felt shame of what they could not possibly help, as when they broke the only saucepan in the house and had to borrow one.

Public houses were allowed to open far into the night and all night at this period, and children of any age were allowed to go in and out of them: often have I gone to the Woodboy public house for a farthing's worth of small beer.

We all had smallpox, and one of us died, and then father began to drink more: and as if dirt and dinginess, bickerings, hidings, rags and assaults of vermin were not hell enough, we were also afeared of the Devil, that 'Enemy of Mankind' invisible but always at our elbow whispering in our ear. When this frightened us, we knelt down and recited the Rosary and invoked our patron saints and guardian angels.

The rear of three one up, one down houses on Archdeacon Lane. These houses had no windows in the back walls, which were only 4½ inches thick from the footings to the eaves. The common tap in the yard was fixed near the gully. (Leicester City Council)

The back of Court D, Archdeacon Lane, looking towards Archdeacon Lane from the common yard. On the right-hand side is No. 84, which was originally two houses, while No. 86 takes in the portion at the bottom of the cul-de-sac and also the left-hand wing. The back lower rooms were dark. The common tap is fixed on the small outbuilding in the background and the waste water had to flow down the open channel approximately 30ft to the gully. (Author)

Above: The Archdeacon Lane Baptist Church was on the corner of Thames Street. As the slums were cleared it lost its congregation and the last service was held in 1938.

Below: Navigation Street in the early 1950s. Pre-war clearance had left vacant lots, which soon acquired the detritus of 'modern' life. (The Leicester Mercury)

In 1891, No. 32 Caroline Street was occupied by Keziah Lang, who was a laundress. She was a widow and lived there with her five children. This photograph was taken in the 1930s and the mangle is still in use. In 1937, of the six people who lived here, five were rehoused by the Council on Iliffe Road. Note the dark interior, low ceilings and 4½in thick single brickwork. The house was demolished in 1940. (Author)

Foundry Square, c.1938. This little group of houses and shops between Queen Mary Street and Foundry Lane was built before St Mark's Church. Next to Willett's fruit merchant was the Earl of Cardigan public house, which was formerly the Waterworks Tavern. (Leicester City Council) Inset: On the right is the rear of Nos 7–13 Foundry Lane, the bedrooms of which overlooked this yard. The entrance from Foundry Lane was by the wide covered entry seen on the right, between Nos 11 and 13, and St Mark's Church can be seen in the background. These slums were demolished in 1944. (Author)

Above: Nos 1–4, Court A, Queen Mary Street. This street led off Foundry Square, which was on the town side of St Mark's Church. The two doors on the left and right are Nos 8 and 10 Queen Mary Street, which were back-to back houses. Apparently the tenants had to walk 60 to 80ft for water or to dispose of any rubbish or waste water. The building with the white wall was a slaughterhouse. (Author)

Below: The rear of Court A. The lady holding an aspidistra may well be moving out prior to demolition. (Leicester City Council)

Above: The back kitchen of No. 8 Queen Mary Street. This photograph was taken on a sunny day from the doorway of the front living room and shows the lack of proper light in the back kitchen. Note the copper, small low window, fireplace, cooking utensils and low ceiling. There was no sink or internal water supply. The two people living here were rehoused on Peake Road in the Northfields estate in 1937 and the houses were demolished the following year.

Left: There were seven houses in Dyers Yard, which was situated off Belgrave Road. It was reached through a long, narrow approach that was opposite the Great Northern Station (today the site of Sainsbury's supermarket). This view looks out from Belgrave Road towards Spittelhouse Street and the canal. The wide gateway on the left led to a common yard at the rear. The factory at the bottom of the yard appears to be disused and the fence on the right-hand side is a hoarding. The tenants were rehoused in 1937 on Hand Avenue and Victoria Road East. (Author)

The Highcross Street–Causeway Lane area from the 1889 25 inch Ordnance Survey map.

Looking towards the junction of St Peter's Lane and Highcross Street in May 1913. The tall, buttressed house, No. 71 Highcross Street, was demolished to widen this very narrow part of St Peter's Lane. The man with the measure is standing next to the rear of the Railway Hotel. This street is now one of the entrances to the Highcross Shopping Centre.

Music and Friends

William Gardiner, 1838.
From the mediaeval period onwards, Highcross Street was the main north-south thoroughfare of the town. From the 1830s, a good deal of working-class housing went up in this quarter. Half-timbered buildings were frequently cleared to make way for the brick-built workers' cottages. Lying on slightly elevated ground, this area was not subject to flooding. The slum clearance programme swept much of the housing away and the old street pattern did not survive the construction of the central ring road in the 1960s.

William Gardiner (1770–1853) was a leading Leicester citizen who was known as a hosiery manufacturer, musician and dilettante. When Joseph Haydn visited London he sent him a present of cotton stockings, the finest it was possible to make, with the name Joseph Haydn embroidered on them in the same thread. He was the brother-in-law of the leading radical and Inspector of Nuisances, George Bown.

The vacant ground that lies between High Street and Sanvey Gate was covered with churches, monasteries and hospitals and at the demolition of these religious houses large spaces were thrown open, which afterwards were converted into orchards and gardens. At the time the art of making bricks was not known and these tracts were enclosed in every direction by walls made of mud and straw, forming dark and gloomy lanes. I remember, as a boy, the frightful sensations I had in an evening when passing through these dismal purlieus. Within the last 20 years the mud walls have begun to disappear and houses for working people give a more cheerful aspect to this solitary part of the town.

The rear of Nos 26, 28 and 30 White Street, which were one up and one down houses, built with walls of single-brick thickness. There were seven houses in this yard and the covered entry leading into the yard is through the doorway in the far corner. The wall at the bottom of the yard belongs to No. 44 Grape Street. The houses in the yard were served by a common tap adjoining the only gully for all the yard drainage and foul water. The slabbing in the foreground leads to the common wash house and WCs. These houses were demolished in 1938. (Author)

St Peter's Cottages at the rear of No. 24 St Peter's Lane. Note the buttressed house behind the washing.

Growing up in West Short Street by Mrs Iris Hall (née Gilbert)

Leicester Oral History Archive, 1983.
Mrs Hall grew up in West Short Street, which ran between White Street and Vine Street, off Causeway Lane. Her father was unemployed, except for when he was taken on by the Corporation as a street sweeper.

You used to step straight in from the street to the living room. A wooden table stood in the middle and there was the old fire grate with hobs and ovens and a sink in the corner which did for everything. There was no kitchen, it was not even curtained off. There was a very cold brick stone floor which you had to scrub – you could not put lino down. This floor was covered by peg rugs which were made by my dad. He did all the cooking and tucked us in at night. There was just one bedroom upstairs. Old wooden stairs with no carpet on led to the single bedroom…We used to have a big double bed one end and another one the other, I suppose that was my mum and dad's, and there were three of us then – three in a bed. I can remember the baby must have slept with my mum and dad, because there was no way you could have got a cot in. In fact, we never used to be able to get out of bed normal like we do now – we had to clamber over the other beds. That was all it was: one up and one down – everything in the one room…

Cinema was a treat on Saturday – going to the twopenny rush. When we got home mum and dad would be perhaps getting up. The tin bath was kept in the wash house and we used to go out the back for water which we shared with eight families. There were five of us in the one house.

[My father] he was the one who looked after us while mother went out working all day…He was known as the cobbler, if kids' shoes wanted mending, they used to send

Cleaning the step of No. 10 St Peter's Cottages, St Peter's Lane. These small houses had a huge factory girder in front of the bedroom windows. Many houses in St Peter's Lane were scheduled for demolition in 1934, but the landlords successfully appealed against their demolition in the County Court. They were eventually demolished in 1938.

round for my dad. He used to earn a few extra coppers that way. He also used to go round the houses with a barrow and they would give him things to take to a pawn shop on Sanvey Gate for 2d or 3d. There was another neighbour, he was the one who cut your hair with the aid of a basin.

I know we all seemed to have a lot of aunts and uncles, but when we grew up they were no relation. They used to take it in turns to take the kids out. It was a community and they all chipped in. They would take it in turns to fetch the coke and dish it out in buckets. The grannies in those days used to sit outside in the street with caps on and with big aprons. All the ladies seemed old: there were no young looking mothers, I suppose it was all the hard work.

Left: The Causeway Lane entry to Bishop Terrace, Court B, in the 1930s. This was situated in a yard at the rear of the old Bishop Blaize public house. This access was by a covered entry between the pub and No. 54. The middle door on the right-hand side of the entry was to a one-roomed dwelling on the first floor occupied by two men. These houses were demolished in 1940. (Author)

Below: The common yard used by the tenants of Bishop Terrace, looking towards the entrance from Causeway Lane. There were nine single houses of the back-to-back or rear wall blank type and six through houses in this court. At the time of this photograph, some of the houses were being used as a store by the adjoining brass foundry. The large gable wall in the middle background is the back of the Bishop Blaize public house. The common tap can be seen fixed against the corner of the public house wall to the right of the girl. Three WCs were located through the open doorway on the left of the photograph. (Author)

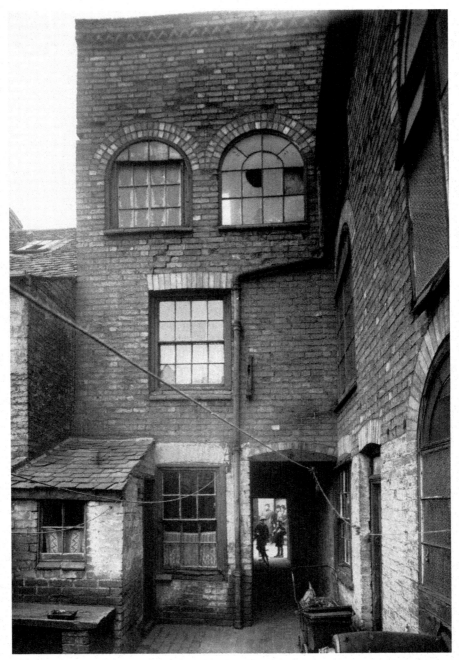

The rear of Nos 40 and 40½ Causeway Lane, c.1937. On the right of the photograph is the rear of a disused chapel, which had been converted into factory premises. The room with the semicircular windows and brick arches was not part of the dwelling on the left, but was interlocked with the factory. This house was demolished in 1940. (Author)

Above: Nos 24–28 Causeway Lane were situated opposite the old maternity hospital and were demolished in 1939. They may have been built in the 18th century and originally overlooked the meadows down to the River Soar. (Author)

Below: Gardening in the common yard at the rear of Nos 24–26. The brickwork of these houses was very dilapidated and was only 4½in thick above plinth course, where there were small bedroom windows. (Author)

Above: Nos 38–42 Vauxhall Street. This street ran from Causeway Lane to St Peter's Lane and these houses were built with 4½in thick, single-brick walls. Buttresses and tie rods were added to prevent the walls bulging. Like many yards, the walls were limewashed in a vain endeavour to reflect light into living rooms that were overshadowed by the closely spaced back projections. These houses were probably due to be demolished in 1934, but were temporarily 'saved' after court action by the owners. Eventually they were demolished in June 1940. (Author)

Below: Nos 22–28 Vauxhall Street. These almshouses (Mason's Charity) had no secondary means of access and were found to be very damp. The date stone of 1832 is clearly visible. (Author)

Above: Nos 123–129 Highcross Street early in 1938. These four houses were three-storeys high at the front and two at the back and were thought to be 400 years old. They have the typical round chimneys of older Leicester housing. No. 125 (left) had a large, carved oak beam across the front room ground floor ceiling, which was thought to have been taken from a previously demolished church. This was probably St Peter's, which stood between Highroads Street and West Bond Street. When it was pulled down in 1573 it also provided building materials for the Free Grammar School. No. 129 was only one room deep, being built up to the back wing of No. 131 Highcross Street. Access to the yard at the rear was by way of a very dark winding passage with three steps up to the back door in the yard. The back portions were covered with Swithland slates. The doors

and windows are taped up to prevent the escape of gas during fumigation. The date on the film poster is Monday 28 February. (Author)

Above: The rear of Nos 123–127 Highcross Street. The open door second from the left is the covered entry leading to the front street. (Author). Below right: A flashlight photograph of the dark, twisted passage in No. 129. There were three steps down from the yard level leading to the ground floor living room at the front. (Author). Below left: In the far corner is the entrance to the dark passage. This dark house was interlocked with No. 131. (Author)

The junction of Highcross Street and Blue Boar Lane in September 1961. (The Leicester Mercury)

Court A, Highcross Street was a row of 12 cottages that lay between Sanvey Gate and All Saints' Church. The view on the left is looking towards Elbow Lane Board School. The photograph on the right shows the very narrow back passage at the rear of these houses and their lack of proper rear windows.

Cumberland Street – a view from Highcross Street towards Long Lane, c.1937. Cumberland Street was 24ft wide and Long Lane was 16ft wide reducing to 10ft. The tenants were rehoused in 1938 and the houses demolished in 1940. (Author)

Diary of a Leicester Factory Hand

Tom Barclay, The Wyvern, *14 December 1894.*

MONDAY: Got up late; lost 'a quarter;' was threatened with 'the rush'. Never could get up after having a drop of beer the night before. Think I shall have to take Wicks's advice and be teetotal.[1] Was a bit of meat for dinner: I like Mondays for that.

TUESDAY: All right this morning; not 'rotten' like yesterday. More meat for dinner; old woman's been to pop.[2] Notice of half-time at the place after this week.

WEDNESDAY: Meat at dinner 'beautifully less'; nippers truff like young ravens.

THURSDAY: Meat nil. Butter ditto. Tea, toast and lard for dinner. Roll on time to Saturday!

FRIDAY: Walked round table at dinner time. Begged a smoke when got to factory. Capital thing 'bacca is to stay hunger. Was a little loaf, but nippers worried it; and missis is suckling.

SATURDAY: Went into The Workman's Brutalizer soon as I reckoned. Was very hungry when went in, not having any grub for nearly 24 hours – only tea and 'bacca. Stomach being empty, soon got boozed. Missis tracing me all over town. Found me and begun to tongue-bang me before company. Went home and slept with head on table. Missis paid shop, went

---

1. William Wicks was a leader of the local temperance movement. He was a Unitarian and was active in adult education and the campaign against the Boer War. He was known as a writer and speaker and was famous for his kindness.
2. The pawnbroker.

City Wall Street ran from Long Lane towards Sanvey Gate, which can be seen through the narrow entry next to the slaughterhouse. The two children are standing next to the entrance to the slaughterhouse yard, which was probably on the line of the old mediaeval wall (This would have run at right angles to the street). These houses consisted of just a living room and bedroom. Those on the right-hand side had a cement plinth, which was an attempt to prevent rising dampness in the external wall. The windows are taped for fumigation and the houses were demolished in 1938, not long after this photograph was taken. The street no longer exists. (Author).

up market, came back and wakened me to beef steaks and mashed potatoes. Gave the children coppers; went up town with Missis. She begged of me not to spend every farthing this week. Got playing 'crib' among some shopmates at The Tom-fool's Rest. Quarrelled with a chap about a deal; went into street and pulled off coat to fight. 'Bobby' came and threatened to run me in. Old gel just came in nick of time to prevent me getting shopped. True what proverb says, 'The grey mare is often the best horse.' Took a bottle of beer home – in spite of all she could do to prevent me. Fetched a neighbour in and we sat soaking and singing: *Comrades, Polly Perkins, Good Old Jeff, Knocked 'em in the Old Kent Road, Old John Barleycorn* and *At Trinity Church I met my doom.* Missis cried; kids were wakened by the singing. Got a fair ' blinder' on. Daylight coming on when I stumbled up to bed.

SUNDAY: Awful headache. Lie abed till bells ring for church. Drink gingerbeer, eat mussels, bathe head. Got the 'jerks'. Opening time; must have 'a hair off the dog that bit me'. The homeopaths are right, 'like cures like' for the time being, at least. Begin to feel right again gradually, but no appetite; could not look at the pudding at dinner, and had to keep out of sight of the fat. Washed and went a walk after tea, and listened to the anarchists in the Gate. What rot! Do not know whether I shall not join the 'Sallys'. Only a tanner in the house. Missis swears she never went round my pockets, though Jack Bounder says he is sure somebody must have 'run the rule over me'. I have never known the Missis to go 'through' me when I have been 'tol-loll'. No money for coal, schooling, rent, or insurance man; nothing only grub. Lets see what we can do next week!

Long Lane was a very narrow street, just 10ft wide, which ran parallel to Sanvey Gate and led from Cumberland Street across Burgess Street and into an even narrower passage called Olive Hill. This photograph shows the houses following fumigation in February 1938. The iron stanchions were there to prevent access by vehicles. In the middle left of the photograph there is a shop where a woman can be seen. These houses were demolished in 1939. (Author)

Durham Street has now disappeared. This view is from Olive Street looking towards Olive Hill, which was a narrow, winding passage running from Junior Street. The 1885 OS map shows Durham Street as a residential street with no factory. The development of Messrs A. and W. de St Dalmas chemical warehouse on the right soon overshadowed these small houses, which were also hemmed in by factories at the rear. This street is now under the apartments of Leicester Square at the junction of St Margaret's Way and Vaughan Way, on the site of the former Richard Roberts factory. (Author)

The Northgate Street area before the coming of the Great Central Railway from the 1889 25in Ordnance Survey map.

The noise of passing trains must have dominated Northumberland Terrace or Court D, Northgate Street. Part of the terrace had to be demolished to make way for the Great Central Railway. The 10ft-wide entry to the terrace lay beneath the railway viaduct running across Northgate Street (just behind where the photographer stood to take this picture). There were 13 single rear wall blank-type houses in the yard along with wash houses, and there was a common tap fixed near the corner of the boundary wall lower down the yard. The terrace stretched from Northgate Street to the junction of Old Mill Lane and Northumberland Street. From Old Mill Lane the yard could be reached through a 5ft-wide covered passage between Nos 24 and 26, which are seen in the distance. The terrace still appeared on Ordnance Survey maps in the 1950s. (Author)

Glimpses of Leicester Slums: Northgate Street

Tom Barclay, The Wyvern, 2 November 1894.

In this season of social and political agitation and contention, and while so many public men are discussing the better housing of the people, I offer your readers a little sketch of that slice of Leicester known as Northgate Street. It extends from Sanvey Gate to Frog Island, but is only 200 yards long: I wish it to be particularly remembered that it is only 200 yards long. Go through almost any morning from 10 to 11 o'clock and you will see something that ought to be described by a realistic French novelist. At this time the street is very much alive with female forms, working women who fill the causeways, accosting one another, chatting to one another; in caps, in hoods, with shawls over their heads, baskets in their hands, and toddling smudge-faced bairns at their apron strings. They saunter in and out the shops, cheapening and chaffering; tidy, tattery, slattern, and scant of clothing. Very few though are ragged. Here are three

103

Looking towards the shopfronts in Northgate Street through an arch of the Leicester viaduct, April 1959. This is possibly the entrance to Court D, shown on the previous page.

butchers' shops all next door to one another: the cuts are not the prime sort, they look scraggy and bemauled. Shopfronts are dingy, grimy, blackened by friction; eggs and bacon are seemingly in great demand here, the glistening kipper too, and the blowsy bloaters enrich the breeze with their robust perfume, and pawnbrokers hang out their clobber on the outward walls.

The women continue to pass and re-pass, and one says to himself 'What a teeming population: wherever can they all come from?' till suddenly he thinks of the courts. My wonder subsided when I counted from A to R on the right, reckoning from Sanvey Gate, and from T to X on the right, reckoning from Frog Island: 18 on one side, five on the other – 23 in the space of 200 yards! In the same space there are eight public houses, three of them with liquor-vaults attached. The brass-barred doors of a couple of these latter being pushed open by mischievous youths as I passed, I beheld groups of women pouring internal libations from small crystal chalices. I supposed them to be engaged in some occult superstitious mystery, but a friend who accompanied me said they were only necking the ordinary morning two-penn'orth of rot-gut. I know not whether 'tis but a small proportion of women who meet thus, or if they meet only on the Monday morn, after the Sunday 'tugs' have been 'shopped' at mine uncles[1] but this I know, and know full well, that if I lived up one of those courts, in a stuffy, smoky, two-roomed little crib, I might be tempted to go to some kind of anodyne[2] or nepenthe[3] for surcease[4] of sorrow. We can not be too careful in ascertaining whether a desire to drink is the cause of the slum, or whether the slum is the cause of the desire to drink.

---

1. *mine uncles*: the pawnbrowker.
2. *anodyne*: serving to assuage pain.
3. *nepenthe*: a drug destroying sorrow.
4. *surcease*: to put an end to.

Above: Looking north, the bowstring girder bridge that carried the Great Central Railway across Northgate Street nearing completion, c.1897. This huge structure shows how the railways could dominate and change the Victorian landscape. It was demolished in July 1981.

Below: Looking down Northgate Street at the junction with Northgate Lane, c.1895. The shop window advertises the Manchester, Sheffield and Lincolnshire (railway) sales. Presumably, the property had been compulsorily purchased for demolition before the building of the Great Central Railway. The long exposure required for this photograph has turned the passers-by into ghosts.

Sanvey Gate in the 1890s, looking towards St Margaret's Church from Northgate Street.

North Gate and Sanvey Gate

Tom Barclay, The Wyvern, *21 June 1895.*

Lest any of your readers, working class or middle class, should think that I take a mean advantage of the slum-dwellers, let me hasten to explain that my business takes me into the courts and alleys. I am no Paul Pry, or spy sent out to spy out the land, and I must repeat what I said in a previous article – that I set down nought in malice.

If I paint some foibles of poor people, that does not prevent me from seeing and knowing that they are the salt of the earth. I am of that class myself and all my sympathies are with it and ever will be, I trust. 'But why not describe the middle class?' I may be asked. Well, in the first place, I have no access to the villas of Stoneygate and the grand houses of the New Walk; then again, I question if there would be the same interest attaching to villadom as to slumdom. We are all interested, or should be, in ridding our land of hunger and dirt and ignorance and hideousness, and to foster this interest is, I take it, one of the objects of these articles; but poverty and hideousness do not exist among the well-to-do.

Saturday last I threaded the purlieus of Sanvey Gate and North Gate, and was repaid, apart from business, by the variety and the bustle of the life around me. We are very much alive 'down the North', I can tell you; and if you are in the dumps come and mix with us, and we will impart to you a smattering of 'the wild joys of living'. In this quarter I am always reminded of Nottingham, which, by general consent, is voted a faster and livelier town than ours. Here are young girls in their swarf-stained calico or linen 'overalls' that they wear in the wool factories. They are cleaning windows, their plump arms bare to the elbows, and they look much prettier than they imagine in this garb that shows the proportion of their figures and calls to mind the drapery of Greek statuary. The efforts of these daughters of our proletariat to adorn the home are both pathetic and beautiful. After the drudgery of the factory they go home and scrub and swill, dust and rub, until everything is like a new pin. Vases are purchased and filled with grasses and flowers to stand on shelves and dressers, and

Court P was located on the north side of Sanvey Gate, near Craven Street. The covered entry to Sanvey Gate was between Nos 53 and 55, while on the left can be seen No. 1 Court P, which was back-to-back with No. 53 and had a distinctive round chimney stack. At the bottom of the yard, from where this photograph was taken, were Nos 2, 3, and 4 Court P. The common tap to these houses is fixed on the wall of the high building on the left, which was the chemist shop on the corner of Craven Street. The gully in the middle of the yard took all the foul surface water away. The tenants of this court were rehoused on Woodshawe Rise in 1938 and the yard was demolished in 1940. (Author)

if we never heard of Rembrandt, or Rosa Bonheur, or Turner, or Dawson we have got hanging up a couple of bright-coloured almanacs and maple-framed prints, *Ecce Homo* and *The Little Sleeper* – angels, shadowy-formed and gauze-clad, bending and smiling above the slumbering baby. In some houses the chest of drawers came up to within 6in of the open door, so small was the house room, but still things were clean; but in other houses everything was mucky, and the trail of the drunkard was over them all – or nearly. For sad bickerings and objurgations could be heard as you passed the door.

'If we had to get through on what you bring we should look blue,' or 'Ah, well, you tek it somewhere else,' (here a gruff male voice mumbles from a recess something about 'more next week'), 'Adjective next week; we've got to live this week. You stick to it, I tell you, and see if you can do better than me; I'm sick of it.'

Alfred Cottages, in a court opposite Craven Street, Sanvey Gate, are a surprise for their cleanliness and bright patches of garden. Close to is the Mission Hall, which has a Working Men's Association.

In North Gate stand three butchers' shops all in a row. This thoroughfare is one of the best in Leicester, a shopkeeper tells me; they are all shops in the front and courts at the back. Two or three of these shops make a show of bacon, piled up in the windows 20-pig strong.

Above: The rear of Nos 3–6 Old Mill Lane, which faced on to Old Mill Lane between Northumberland Street and Berkley Street. The range of WCs in the middle background were common to the yard and gave no privacy. Passing along behind the WCs to the left is the approach to Nos 7 and 8, Court E. The houses standing in the background are Berkley Cottages. Tenants were rehoused on Limber Crescent in 1938 and the houses demolished in 1939. (Author)

Certain houses and shops are bunged up, the new track of the M.S. and L. railway is going to cut through them, and we shall have a bridge over the street. Part of Court D is coming down; it is the largest court I have yet sampled, and is called Northumberland Terrace at the end of Craven Street, where it comes through. Several North Gate courts astonish you by bending round at right angles into Sanvey Gate again.

And where do all these people work, for they are as numerous and as busy as ants under a stone in the woods? At Collyer's, at Forsall's and at Thompson's. An insurance agent, who does business among them, tells me he has few deaths and that the people are tough, in spite of the swarm of factories, in spite of confinement in them, in spite of close courts and in spite of the consumption of bad beer and whisky.

The smudgy 'toddling weans' tumbling about, the women parading four deep on the causeways, butchers and grocers chaffering, 'kids' acting the manly by smoking 'Woodbine' cigarettes, or tossing for coppers in an angle of a wide yard with posts in front, sounds of song from the bars of the numerous vaults and pubs, and flirtation between the aforementioned window-cleaning young girls and their 'chaps' – truly a vast and varied conglomeration and hurly-burly. And what impressed me most of all are the sociability of the people, their relish of life, their spirit of 'Hail-fellow-well-met' and an obvious determination to fulfil the proverb, 'While we live let us live.' I believe there are more members to a family at work in this district than you get in most others; probably, too, work is more constant, wool factories being more regular in giving employment. Where father is a tacker and young Jack sprigs or 'sorts stuff', while mother and eldest daughter work at Thompson's, it is better financially than were none to go to work but father. To me there is something half Irish about the reckless and rollicking North End. To reverse a phrase of Byron's, I think its very human inhabitants are 'linked with one crime and a thousand virtues'.

A Health Inspector making notes in Court R, Sanvey Gate shortly after the properties had been fumigated prior to their demolition. The houses on the right were of the back-to-back type and had no through ventilation. Apparently, a portion of the old city wall was visible in this court, though it is not shown in this photograph, and had been used as a foundation for a brick boundary wall. In January 1938, 11 people were rehoused from this court to Raven Road and Pilkington Road, and the court was demolished later that year. (Author)

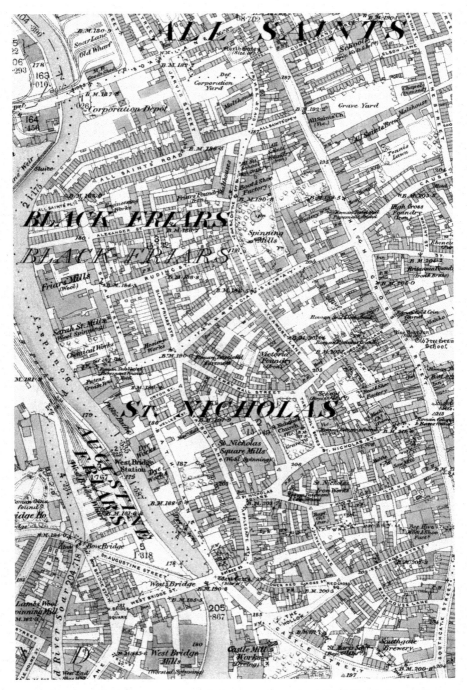

The All Saints, Blackfriars and St Nicholas areas from the 1886 25in Ordnance Survey map.

Thomas Smith's Roman Pavement Hardware store on the corner of Jewry Wall Street and Friars Causeway, c.1896. The pavement remained hidden until 1832, when it was uncovered in the basement of No. 53 Jewry Wall Street, and in 1882 the Council bought the house. Thomas Smith became the pavement's custodian and in 1891 was living at No 53. The map opposite shows the pavement located under the above roadway. Unfortunately, both the shop and the pavement lay in the path of the proposed Manchester, Sheffield and Lincolnshire Railway (later the Great Central Railway).

Jewry Wall Street

Tom Barclay, The Wyvern, 12 July 1895.
This article was written shortly before the arrival of the new railway line.

By the side of St Nicholas's Church and the Jewry Wall runs Jewry Wall Street, in one of the most ancient parts of Leicester. From one end branches off Sycamore Lane, from the other 'The Friars', and the rumbling, wool-spinning factories of Bath Lane and Sarah Street are close by. All Saints and The Pingle are little more than a stone's throw distant, which shows how close west and north once were in our borough. Jewry Wall Street bears on its face every evidence of age, not to speak of decay. The projecting doorsteps, that Mr Jabez Chaplin complained of the other day as likely to cripple blind people, abound here.[1] The courts have wide gateways with heavy wooden beams and many of the windows at the back are the old-fashioned leaded sort.[2] The slums are the slummiest that I have yet been into; not Britannia Street can exceed the squalor of these courts. I spoke about cupboards between Woodboy Street and Britannia Street that looked like a bit of board let into a hole in the wall, but here in Jewry Wall Street are houses without any cupboard at all.

'You have to put all your food on a shelf then?' said I to a woman that I got into conversation with.

---

1. Jabez Chaplin was a leader of the Hosiery Union and one of the founders of the local Independent Labour Party in Leicester. He was subsequently elected as a Councillor.
2. Despite being quite short, Jewry Wall Street had five separate courts of dwellings (Courts A-G).

Demolition in progress at the junction of Talbot Lane, Jewry Wall Street, Friars Causeway and Black Friars Street, c.1896. The new railway required a mile-and-a-half-long viaduct and a station necessitating the demolition of a large number of houses. As the navvies cut a swathe across the area to make way for the mammoth structure, whole streets disappeared. Sycamore Lane, Charlotte Street and Friars Road were lost forever, replaced by the new Great Central Street. Half of Friars Causeway was buried beneath the station and Alexander Street and Ruding Street were truncated to connect with the newly diverted and extended Jarvis Street. Other changes included the severing of Talbot Lane and Jewry Wall Street and the creation of a new thoroughfare with the extension of Welles Street. The horse is pictured outside the shop shown on the previous page.

'Oh,' she answered, 'we daren't put it on the shelf very often; the shelf isn't high enough, you see, and the cats and dogs would soon have it.'

What did the woman do, then? She used an old orange-box, turning the open side to the wall. There was no wallpaper on the walls, and the ceiling was black for the want of whitewash. These cribs are inhabited seemingly by people who are 'down on their luck' and have no chance. The rent of them is only 2s a week. Here in one is a young widow, quite alone in the house, doing washing for a living; in another is a man who was blinded at his trade by an accident. A lot of the property is coming down, as in Northgate Street, to make room for the M.S. and L. railway; but, railway or no, any sanitary inspector who saw these rookeries would condemn them at once. The people must be miserably poor. I never saw in other districts so many people suffering from some physical disability or other, I was reminded of Hogarth's pictures. All seems raggedness, dirt, confusion.

I wonder whether I am boring your middle-class readers by these sketches of 'mean streets', because I must needs be a little monotonous, and I do not wish to be sensational. In this house now, they have been burning wood: can't afford much coal, I suppose. The children have been round the streets and wharves, and into the country lanes for it. The white ash that it leaves in burning is all over the hobs and shelves. In this other house there is but one little three-legged table and two old chairs with the backs broken. I can imagine

The corner of Charlotte Street and Friars Causeway in 1895, shortly before demolition. The posters on the wall are for elections to the Board of Guardians and the School Board. The poster for the Liberal candidates for the guardians, Fullagar, Kemp and Smith, is pasted over one for the Independent Labour Party's School Board candidate Mrs Saunderson, who in 1895 was the first woman ever elected for Labour in Leicester. Fanny Fullagar, a Liberal, was the first woman ever elected to public office in Leicester.

what the bedroom is. The curtains are yellow with dirt; I would not give twopence for what the poor woman has on, and she looks only half alive.

Suppose we change the scene. Ladies and gentlemen, our next picture is of a middle-class family in the vicinity of Stoneygate. The head of the family is an urbane, mellifluous-tongued gentleman who

'rises when he likes himsel',
His flunkeys answer to the bell.'

The maid has been up three hours before him, but she steps gingerly and knocks respectfully at his summons. He has a bath in the bathroom. He descends the carpeted staircase to the breakfast-room. The eggs are of the freshest and the coffee of the richest, and the bacon was not bought at 4d a pound. The groom and coachman are in the stables. The children have been attended to by a nursemaid in the nursery. In the kitchen the cook is already preparing an elaborate dinner of several courses, after which will be served plenty of good, healthy fruit. The housemaid has been dusting and black-leading and polishing. On the walls are real works of art; here is a Dawson, here Copley Fielding; this is a Ward, that is a David Cox.[3] There is blue china, costly ceramic work, rare old lace, artistic embroidery. In the library are the works of Swinburne, William Morris, Pater, Davidson, Ruskin, Hardy, Kipling, Tennyson, Browning, M'Carthy; in short, the best literature.

---

3. Most probably the Nottingham landscape artist Henry Dawson (1811–1878). Antony Vandyke Copley Fielding (1787–1855), commonly called Copley Fielding, was born in Sowerby, near Halifax, and was famous for his watercolour landscapes. David Cox (1783–1859) was another English landscape painter. James Ward, R.A. (1769–1859) was one of the finest animal, portrait and landscape painters of Regency England.

The Blackfriars tessellated Roman pavement was believed to have been constructed between the years ad 70 and 85. Part of the Act passed in 1893 which granted the Manchester, Sheffield and Lincolnshire Railway permission to build the London Extension also legally bound the company to preserve the mosaic and to provide public access to it. To meet this obligation, the company built this tiled chamber beneath the station. Interested observers could also view the mosaic from above through a prismatic glass floor set into the platform itself. It is in the chamber that this photograph was taken. The pavement was removed to the Jewry Wall Museum in the mid-1970s.

The junction of Friars Causeway and Great Central Street, c.1960. Although these houses avoided demolition for the new station in the 1890s, they did not survive the building of the ring road in the 1960s.

Sun Light Cottages, Friars Causeway, c.1895. The house on the right, No. 17, was the home of William Alvey, a shoe finisher, and his four children. The open entry led to Bethel Court where there were 17 people living in four cottages. There is a Council handbill on the wall about summer diarrhoea. Many of the houses on Friars Causeway were back-to-back, with those facing on to courts at the rear, and were some of the many properties which were demolished to make way for the new railway line.

On a Broadwood, or Collard, is a pile of operatic and other music, symphonies, sonatas, cantatas and fantasias. Miss in her teens will play something from these most nights. She has a lithe figure, and a shower of hair that reaches to her waist; her health is as good as her beauty, and she blooms like a rose. I do not envy her, but I wish something could be done towards bringing about as fair a lot for her poor, white-faced sisters of Jewry Wall Street and Britannia Street. Why should she learn French and drawing, and the piano and English grammar, and practice callisthenics, and be able to take a bath every morning, and wear bright, beautiful clothing and change frequently, and breathe plentiful fresh air and have generous foods, while others who work hard have no chance of getting such things. I cannot see the justice of it, and I cannot see the consistency of it with the religion of Christ.

It seems to me that if rich and well-to-do folk did really think we poor were going to sit beside them on thrones in the mansions of the blest they would treat us a little better now. It is impossible for me to think that anyone who refuses to associate with me here, believes that he may have to do so through all eternity. Such people know no more about and feel no more about real Christianity than they do about Mohammedanism or Buddhism. Those supercilious people who will not move in this, that and other 'set' have two alternatives; either to declare their Christianity a sham, or else to dress the same as we poor, come and live among us, work the same as we do, and act and think and feel as though we were all brothers. We do not want to be the same as they are: we have got no respectability or caste-feeling. We will have nothing of that. Until they have got rid of that, we would not mix with them, even if they would with us. We want to be natural and companionable. At present we are very ignorant, but are at least not ignorant enough to think we have a right to despise our fellow creatures because they have not had the opportunities that we have had – often through their enslavement.

Above: Blue Boar Lane in 1938, looking from Great Central Street towards Highcross Street. Blue Boar Terrace (10 houses) stood behind these front houses and access was by a narrow passage where the two people in the photograph are standing. The three-storey houses on the left (Nos 21 and 19) were built with single-brick walls. They were demolished in 1938 and the tenants rehoused on Windford Crescent. Below: The large back yard of No. 19 Blue Boar Lane, which was occupied by a chimney sweep for many years.

A tenant standing at the back door of No. 5 Blue Boar Lane. The covered entry led from the front street into a common yard shared by five houses. The back walls of the house were fractured and the houses were demolished in 1938. The five residents of No. 5 moved to Heyford Road, on the Braunstone estate.

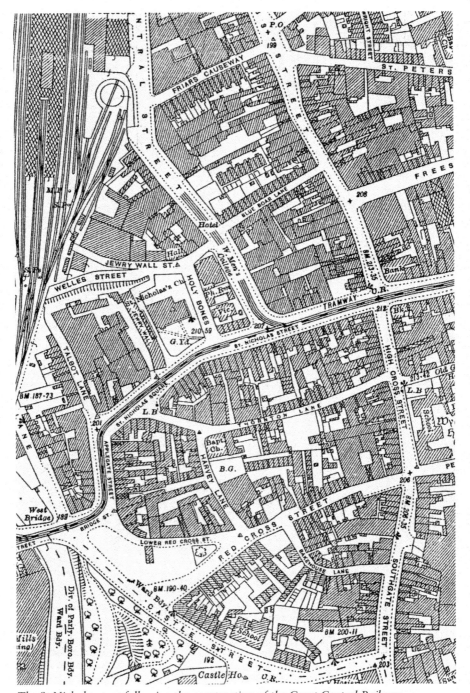

The St Nicholas area following the construction of the Great Central Railway.

A view from the Hollow looking east towards Redcross Street in the distance. The backway is to the Loggerheads public house on Lower Redcross Street. The houses were acquired by the Council in 1897 and subsequently demolished to enable the raising of the street levels. This site is now in Castle Gardens, and the view looks towards the Holiday Inn.

The people in this queue in Redcrosss Street have come to sell their woollen rags to A.E. Piggot and Sons scrap merchants. In the early 1950s, scrap merchants gave good money for old rags. A temporary wall hides the site where several houses with courts behind had been cleared in the pre-war years.

Redcross Street: looking west from Highcross Street towards West Bridge. The peace poster seen on No. 6 Redcross Street is from the 1931 general election. On the right, beyond the factory, there were three covered entries to a maze of courtyard dwellings going through to Thornton Lane.

Filthy Hovels

Cllr T.J. Gooding, Leicester Mercury, 1 June 1932.
In June 1932, the Council approved the demolition of 112 houses in Thornton Lane, Redcross Street, Bakehouse Lane and Havey Lane. Many of the houses had low ceilings and small rooms and were built in courtyards, overshadowed by factories. The ravages of time had left these small homes with bulging brickwork, uneven floors, leaking roofs and rising damp. Following a two-hour inspection, Cllr T.J. Gooding said that he was forced to the conclusion that demolition was long overdue.

I have been in houses today which I call filthy hovels. I would not put a dog in some of these places. It is all very well talking about financial strategy, but my heart goes out to those in distress, and when I see a wrong that ought to be righted, I say it ought to be done. No doubt in the past those people who owned those houses reaped a rich harvest…

Palaces

W.T. Coltman, president of the Leicester Property Owners, Leicester Mercury, 8 February 1933.

The very worst slums in Leicester are palaces compared to such places as the Isle of Dogs in London. We are combating the alleged slum area in Redcross Street, because there are a number of houses in the area which ought not to be pulled down at all. There is no overcrowding.

Redcross Street: looking east towards Peacock Lane and the William Shipley Ellis memorial wing of the old Alderman Newton's School.

Poison Gas Plant

Leicester Mercury, *Friday 19 October 1934.*
On the morning of the move to the new house, a Corporation furniture van called to collect the furniture and belongings of the slum dwellers. These were taken to one of two isolated 'defesting' stations, where the van and its contents were subjected for four hours to a dose of deadly hydrocyanic gas to kill off lice and bugs. Before demolition, as a matter of course, the old houses were also fumigated with gas to prevent the dissemination of vermin through the sale of old woodwork for firewood. Hydrogen cyanide (under the brand name Zyklon B) was employed by the Nazi regime in its gas chambers. It is still used for executions in the United States.

Leicester Health Committee have set up a poison gas plant with which they propose to fumigate Leicester's slums. Hydrocyanide gas, which is very deadly, is to be used, and the gas will be emitted from a van into houses in the Redcross street area, starting next week.

Men will work in gas masks, with oxygen cylinders handy in case of emergency. Owing to the fact that hydrocyanic gas cannot be detected by smell, warning notices will be put up around the area to ensure safety. All furniture, bedding and household belongings are to be treated with this gas before the people move into their new homes on the Freakes estate.

The cottages will be defested by injection of the gas after all windows, doorways, chimneys etc., have been sealed. The chimney pots will then be unsealed and the gas, which is lighter than air, allowed to escape.

121

This photograph was part of a set of magic lantern slides for lectures given on behalf of the Garden Cities and Town Planning Association. It was used as an example of poor planning and housing conditions. The central drawing, published overleaf by the Leicester Pioneer in 1902, seems to be based on this photograph. Given that the other two drawings were taken from Southgate Street, it could be assumed that this photograph was taken in that vicinity, and could even be another view of Court A. These courts were demolished in 1926 to make way for the Southgate bus station.

THE LEICESTER PIONEER
OF SOCIAL PROGRESS.

No. 78.   Post Free 6/6 per Year.   Registered as a Newspaper.   SATURDAY, DECEMBER 6th, 1902.   ONE PENNY.

For the CHEAPEST and BEST CLOTHING—BOWLES & BOWLES, 7, HAYMARKET, also BELGRAVE GATE.

Scenes in Leicester
Slumland.

The Warrens of the Poor, F.W. Rogers

Leicester Pioneer, 20 September 1902 (excerpt).
The Leicester Pioneer *had been founded by Tom Barclay in the early 1890s. Ten years later, F.R. Rogers and the Secularist F.J. Gould were involved with rejuvenating the paper. The paper publicised the Garden Cities movement and Gould attended several of its meetings. It also printed a series of articles by F.W. Rogers on Leicester's slums. His condemnation of the slums as 'dens where morality is impossible' echoes the moralistic tone of Joseph Dare, rather than the humanity of Barclay.*

Was it Carlyle who charged the people of England with paying far more attention to the breed of their horses than of their men? When I saw a dirty-looking urchin, not yet out of its babyhood, squirming in a filthy gutter, with a look of animal contentment on its villainous face – yes, its villainous face – for, barely two years old, it had the hallmark of the criminal upon it – when I saw it, I set to work to find in what kind of soil this choice plant was nurtured.

I have found it and sampled it, and when anyone next tells me there are no slums in Leicester, I will pity him for his ignorance. Slums? They tell us London, Liverpool and Birmingham can rival us in this particular. Possibly so, but there are dens in our own town where morality, or any other virtue, is impossible. This is not hearsay. I have visited these places, gone into the houses – (I nearly said homes) – measured their rooms, heard some of their tales and come away sick at heart.

Do you want to know where they are, and who derives revenue from some of these glorified pig-sties? I could tell you both, but sufficient as to the latter if I say that these owners pass as 'honourable men'. Some of their names are prominent in the civic life of Leicester, and I am sorry to say some are prominent in the religious life as well. Take Newton Ward first then, and the reader may recognise the places if he can. There are courts in Newton Ward where even the gas at cost representative of that district would find it hard to retain his respectability.

Here is one. There are not many houses in it, and the rents are high, viz 1s 6d per week, which is about three times more than they are worth. One room up and one down does

123

Looking west from St Nicholas Street towards St Nicholas Square at its junction with Thornton Lane, c.1900. The pub on the left is the Northampton Arms.

not offer much scope for physical recreation. The drawing-room of one establishment measured 12½ft by 10½ft, which gives a floor space of 131ft 3in, the height of the room being 8ft 6in this would give a total cubic [measurement of] 1,115 cubic feet. In one of the houses a woman and two young boys lived, which gives them an average air space of 371 cubic feet each. There is nothing deducted here for tables, chairs and the ordinary furniture of the room which will be underestimated if taken at 60ft. This would give a total area of 1,055ft, which comes out per head of the inhabitants at 351 cubic feet. The local government board regulations for lodging house room is 400 cubic feet per person, while prisoners in their cells are allotted 800 cubic feet each. How much healthier would these people be in gaol.

Getting into conversation with one of the women, whose husband was at the war (happy man), I elicited her opinion of the dwellings. 'No room to wash,' she said, 'no room to do nothing, no room to stand; and as you lie in bed you can see the sky through the roof.' The washing was, of course, done in the yard, one reason being that the only tap to the houses was there; and for the other reason cited – that there was nowhere else to do it. Oh sublime existence.

The next visit was to a larger court and was approached through a dark, narrow passage. One or two beetle-browed men looked suspiciously at the stranger, but vouchsafed no conversation. The rents of these houses varied from as low as 1s 3d per week up to 3s 8d, varying according, I suppose, to the amount of cubic feet of space allotted for habitation. Some were two-roomed houses, a few had three rooms, and in two cases, at least, it rose to the luxury of four rooms. In one house, containing two bedrooms and a sitting room, so called (though, personally, I would have preferred to sit in the Abbey Park), there lived a man and woman, a boy of 14 and a girl of eight. I have been trying hard ever since to solve the problem as to how they divided themselves up at night, so that neither the boy nor the girl should sleep in the same room or in the room of the elder people. Possibly a bed was provided downstairs, as appeared to be the case in several

124

SATURDAY, JUNE 23rd, 1934   THE ILLUSTRATED LEICESTER CHRONICLE 5

LEICESTER'S SLUM RACKET EXPOSED

Scandalous Profiteering In Rents
From Poverty-Stricken Families

Miserable Dwellings Exploited
By Speculators

HORRORS OF SLUMLAND

Profiteering and speculation in Leicester's slums with ruthless disregard for the unfortunate people who have to live in the hovels, has become a big business. Scandalous rents for ramshackle and filthy houses are bringing rich incomes for the investors, and in the last few months the "racket" has grown out of all proportions. The misery of the poor is being exploited on a financial basis. "Rack-renting" and "farming-out," and the speculation in slums that are likely to be demolished are features of this inhuman business. Meanwhile, the Slum Sub-Committee of the City Corporation has prepared a scheme for the demolition of the worst slums in Leicester. In the Britannia-street—Woodboy-street area over 420 houses are doomed, and escape from dirt and gloom made possible for 1,502 men, women and children. The terrible and incredibly filthy homes of the slum dwellers are described below.

There are hundreds of hovels like this in the heart of the city.

This excerpt is from an exposé of the speculators who were acquiring slum property in the hope that they could cash in when the cleared land was sold for industrial use, June 1934.

instances. In that event the bed may have been used as a table, otherwise it is hard to say where the table would have been placed.

Another house, a two-roomed one, contained a woman, a girl of 21 and a boy of 14. Where do they sleep? Two shillings per week was paid for this establishment. Anyone who has been compelled, owing to indisposition, to take every meal in a bedroom, if in addition to that was forced to put up with all the work of the house, washing, cooking, cleaning etc., being done in the same apartment, will agree with me that neither the meal time nor the sleeping time would be a very pleasantly expected period of the day. In some of the cases cited, there is a reasonable supposition that work brought from a factory may form a still further item of domestic diversion, carried on in that parlour bedroom.

The worst of these slums are reached through covered passages leading from narrow streets. The houses surround a cobbled court: sunless, insanitary and evil-smelling. Their only note of cheer is the shrill laughter of pale-faced urchins playing in gutter filth. The stranger is eyed suspiciously by little knots of raggedly dressed women, whose haggard faces pitilessly reveal their hardships. Through the low and narrow doorways of the houses could be seen men, coatless and collarless, seated on backless chairs and wooden boxes. These slum dwellers themselves gave our reporter a graphic description of their home lives.

It was a story of degradation. In one court, only one couple were man and wife. Illegitimate families, numbering as many as 11 children, contributed to poverty. A wife told of the horrors of her neighbourhood. 'It is terrible how many men are living with

"Back gardens" in slumland. These back entrances are also used.

125

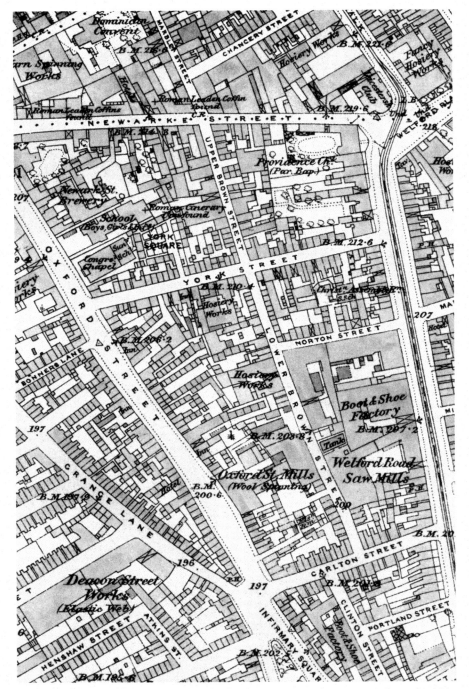

The Grange Lane, Oxford Street, Upper and Lower Brown Street area from the 1886 Ordnance Survey map.

T.J. Painter and Co., pawnbrokers, on the corner of Mill Lane and Grange Lane and seen from Mill Lane in 1956 or 1957. Next to the separate entrance to the pledge office is the entrance to Court A, where there were four houses with a common yard. This corner is now the site of the De Montfort University students' union building.

unmarried mothers in these houses,' she said. 'They are not fit to bring up their own children. The men bring no money to keep the home going and the poor kids are turned out to beg their food from neighbours. We often have to whip round to find them slices of bread. Besides, it is not right for our children to grow up among such shame.'

These tumbling-down buildings are not worthy of the name house. Built over 100 years ago, they are low ceilinged, unventilated and dimly lit. Doorways are only 5ft 2in high and 2ft wide. Ceilings are only 8ft high and in the bedrooms only seven. The stairways are narrow, steep and dark, with no handrails. Houses are built back-to-back, with a wall of only half-a-brick thickness. Windows are tiny, but in many cases the glass and frame have been knocked out to give sufficient ventilation. These windows generally faced north with the result that many of the houses have been perpetually sunless.

Rush-laid floors and ceilings – a feature of Leicester cottages – are the breeding ground of vermin. Sanitary inspectors are unable to rid the houses of fleas, lice and rats. One woman, with tears in her eyes, said that her two sons, who were shop assistants, threatened to leave home because of the cruel jibes of their fellow workers about the vermin they were unable to keep out of their clothing. At one house, the bedroom was so over-run with insects that the occupant – a woman – preferred to sleep in the yard during the summer.

Grange Lane and Oxford Street

Tom Barclay, The Wyvern, 25 July 1895

Grange Lane, pronounced by the inhabitants Green Lane, runs from Infirmary Square to the Newarke, and between Asylum Street and Oxford Street. Towards the Newarke end is a little 'pudding bag' street with the disagreeable name of Pentonville and all its double houses are terribly stuffy, hemmed in and smothered as they are by the back ways of Oxford Street and

The junction of Newarke Street and Oxford Street in January 1900. The bill posters had covered these properties while they were left vacant prior to the widening of Newarke Street. Among those advertised were the celebrated music hall turn 'Casey's Court' at the Palace Theatre and the Christian Socialist Revd Conrad Noel.

Mill Lane. Many of the houses of Grange Lane are but two-roomed, so that the houses of the courts and the street houses are back-to-back; but some courts form squares extending right to the backs of Oxford Street. In one, I found what I had never seen before, a court within a court, and getting into conversation with an old stockinger I used to wind for years ago, I learned that there are three distinct properties up this court.

'They force 'em to whitewash you like this, don't they,' I queried.

'Oh yes; the inspector's been round'.

My informant formerly lived in a house in Redcross Street that had not been whitewashed for eight years, and he could not get the landlord to do anything. Unable to move the landlord, he 'put the sanitary inspector on to it', and things were soon made right.

'But he found out as I'd been to the inspector, and so he gave me notice to leave.'

'But he couldn't turn you out for that, could he?'

'To tell you the truth I wasn't very sorry that he did give me notice. You see, I'd been very bad with rheumatiz; whether it was the house as made 'em worse or not, I don't know: and I owed a bit o' rent. So I cleared out and came down here, and he came down after me.'

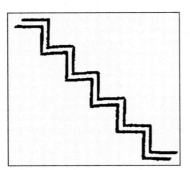

'And did you have to pay?'

'I paid him with my tongue, that was all: I told him he ought to be ashamed of himself, and he was glad to get out of the yard. You're not obliged to pay, you know, when they give you notice like that.'

My stockinger was limping with 'rheumatiz'. A charitable person sent him to Ashby-de-la-Zouch baths (or waters), but he is not cured. In the next court the ' kidney' pavement is half up and the surfaces of the bricks are gone as if they had been eaten away. Rutland Cottages are fairly decent dwellings, but are

Above: Pentonville, off Grange Lane, was built c.1862 by William Dudgeon. This picture was taken in 1959.

reached by a passage. Now comes perhaps the most peculiar thing in building arrangements in all Leicester. A narrow passage that two cannot well walk abreast in, familiarly known as 'the twizzle an' twine', zig-zags from Grange Lane to Oxford Street; a diagram could best explain it to those who have never been through; perhaps your printers can assist me.

Each one of the angles is the corner of a houses and a little yard; I remember a similar but not so tortuous passage which existed in Rutland Street some years ago, on the place now occupied by Exchange Buildings. Oxford Street is wide, and that part next to the Infirmary Square looks like a bit transplanted from old Nottingham. The courts range from A to N and are the most spacious I have yet been in. I do not remember anywhere else beside Oxford Street where the houses on courts are three-storey high.

Above: Gosling Street, off Grange Lane, seen from Pentonville in 1965.

Below: The junction of Mill Lane and Gateway Street (formerly Asylum Street) in 1965. (Newarke Houses Museum)

Men and women sit outside their doors as though they were in the street; you do not catch slum-dwellers doing this often unless the court is large. Another thing I noticed about Oxford Street courts is they are all whitewashed; perhaps it is the whitewashing season. The sanitary inspector has evidently been round; the Medical Officer of Health's admonitions and instructions as to the summer diarrhoea are posted up in every entry, and upper-storey windows are open almost without exception. The walls of houses in 'the twizzle an' twine' above alluded to are also whitewashed, but I would not care to live there. The men about here are gardeners, navvies, costers, bag-coal men and such; they are sturdy of build, hard in texture and well known to the rest of Leicester for their proficiency in the 'noble art of self-defence'. The women stitch gloves and pants. Shoe, hosiery and wool-spinning factories abound in the neighbourhood, and Mr Luke Turner's elastic works hisses distractingly all day long.

On my way back to the centre of the town, I paid a visit to the Labour Club, No. 2, which has just been

The corner of Upper Brown Street and Eaton Square sometime after the October 1900 general election. A Council official holds his measure and the locals pose in front of a selection of largely political posters. A Liberal poster urges voters to vote 'straight' and not to 'plump' – to no avail. In a two-member constituency, the Independent Labour Party candidate, Ramsey Macdonald, split the Liberal vote, thereby enabling the Conservatives to win a seat for the first time in 40 years. Eaton Square was not a square but rather two cul-de-sacs of back-to-back houses, which are now the piazza in front of Phoenix Arts. Enfield Buildings on the other side of Newarke Street is only dimly visible through the haze.

opened in Millstone Lane, in rooms extending over what used to be the People's Mission Hall. Thomas Cooper held meetings in this same hall, I am told, in Chartist times. The club is intended for the better organisation of Castle Ward, to which Orange Lane and Oxford Street belong. Not one of the people sitting in rows outside their houses, whether up courts or not, have I ever found reading a book: this is a significant fact. Papers are read, I find, in nine cases out of 10 for the betting news. If a woman or young girl wants fiction, she never thinks of going to the library for a book; she buys a most trashy novelette at a half-penny or a penny. Now, until people love to read and discuss they must remain ignorant; and while they are ignorant they must be slavish and vulgar, and probably brutal. But if a man has no

Another view of Eaton Square over 30 years later. The pipework suggests that, since the previous photograph, gas light had been installed. These houses were declared unfit for human habitation in 1935. It is possible that these houses were built by Thomas Bland of Lower Redcross Street. Bland was a builder who took every opportunity to cram as many houses as he could on to the sites he developed and the local Board of Health was powerless to stop him. He was elected as a Liberal Councillor in 1863. Not visible in the photograph is a standpipe, which was the sole source of water for these houses. They were demolished in 1937. (Author)

better ideal than dogs, drunkenness, rowdiness and obscenity, is it his fault? If it is his fault, are we to treat him as a lower animal, with whom we can have no comradeship? If it is not his fault, is it your fault? These are questions that require answering. Meanwhile, let me give you a transcript of a conversation I heard in public house close to Infirmary Square. It was during the election, and the parties were evidently trying to get at the meaning of the Independent Labour Party.

'Well, I think they doon't b'lieve in nothink; leastways, I can't understand 'em.'

'Why, you fool, that's them in Humberstone Gate – them a' doon't believe in nowt – Bradlaugh's lot.'[1]

'Well wot are they then; wot do they b'lieve in?'

'It ain't religion, ye donkey, it's labour; they want a fair day's pay for a fair day's work.'

'Well, that's all right, but I was going to say the' is SOMETHIN'; the' must be SOMETHIN'.'

'Must the'? Well, I should like to see him; I think when we're gone from here we're done with.'

'Well, all right, you can 'ave your say, and then ye won't shift me. But I won't argufy no more, cos I've forgot myself, and a public-'ouse ain't no place to argy about such things. Joe, giz a song!'

---

1. Bradlaugh's lot in Humberstone Gate is a reference to the Leicester Secular Society (still going strong), of whom Barclay was a prominent member

An unknown row of cottages (possibly Carlton Cottages off Lower Brown Street), c.1930. The absence of any pipes suggests that these cottages were lit by paraffin lamps. (Author)

Peake's Yard, off Upper Brown Street. Peake's cottages were declared unfit for habitation in 1935, and would have been demolished soon after. Phoenix Arts now stands on this site. (Author)

Above: The junction of Lower Brown Street and Carlton Street in 1965. (Newarke Houses Museum)

Above: Court A, Gray Street, off Mill Lane. Above right: Asylum Street. Bottom right: Jarrom Street looking west towards the Havelock and Clarendon Street junctions in 1964. The houses on the right are now part of the De Montfort University campus, while the site on the left is now part of the Royal Infirmary. Clearance in this area began after 1957 and continued into the late 1960s.

A 1950s view of the junction of Clarendon Street and New Bridge Street, now part of St Andrew's estate. (Newarke Houses Museum)

The horseflesh shop on Waterloo Street in 1918. Horse meat had not been a part of the working-class diet prior to World War One, though food shortages encouraged what were euphemistically called 'Belgian butchers'. Most of the time horseflesh was reserved for pets, even during the rationing in World War Two. The law required that horseflesh could not be sold in an ordinary butchers.

135

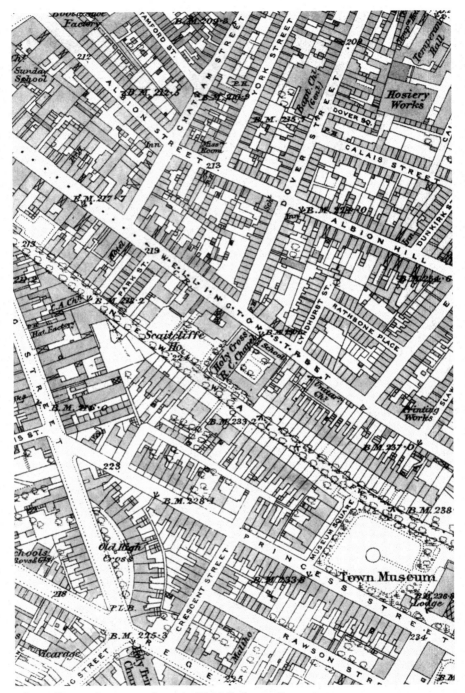

The Wellington Street area from the 1886 Ordnance Survey map.

Above: Court C, Wellington Street was situated close to today's Central Library. In 1832, James Cook had a small workshop over a cowhouse in a yard leading off Wellington Street. On 10 August 1832 he was executed for the murder of Mr Paas, whose remains he attempted to destroy by fire in his workshop. Initially Cook's body was hung in a gibbet on Saffron Lane, but after public protest over this 'barbarous exhibition' his body was removed and buried nearby. Below: Wellington Street on 30 December 1927. Court H and Court E 'Ivy Cottages' lay behind these houses and were reached through narrow entries from the street. The small houses which were on the corner of Wellington and Dover Street were demolished c.1914 to make way for J. Pick's new factory.

A view of the rear of Park Street on the west side taken from the New Walk end of the row. Two WCs are in the foreground with a common tap fixed against the wall (now the Pause Bar). A shared wash house is in the middle of the yard and two more WCs with another tap are at the further end. The tall building in the background is the De Montfort public house, which stands opposite the end of Chatham Street. Although the tenants of the houses were rehoused in 1938, the outbreak of war meant that this street was not demolished until after 1953. (Author)

Above: Close examination of the posters on the wall dates this photograph of Park Street to the summer of 1937. The view is from Wellington Street looking towards New Walk. There were 24 houses in this street with a right of way at the far end into New Walk. A woman is standing at the door of No. 2, and the width of the road was just 18ft. (Author) Below: Although the tenants were rehoused on North Braunstone before the war, this photograph was taken in September 1953. Following their demolition, a garage for the Leicester Mercury was built on the site. This has now gone and has been replaced by a block of Council offices. This was accomplished by moving Park Street so that it now sits on the boundary of Holy Cross Church. (The Leicester Mercury)

The junction of Calais Hill and Calais Street looking from Dover Street and the Dover Castle pub towards the turn into Dunkirk Street. The slaughterhouse on the right may well be the one referred to below. Today the Dover Street car park is on the left of the picture. (Leicester City Council)

The Warrens of the Poor

F.W. *Rogers,* The Leicester Pioneer, 4 *October 1902 (excerpt).*
Even in the 1930s there was still a profusion of slaughterhouses close to housing in the central areas.

There are a number of private slaughterhouses which should have been abolished long ago. Why are they not? The Corporation have powers to abolish them, and surely no one will deny that the proximity of these places to dwelling-houses is inimical to the health of the inhabitants, There is one down in Castle Ward, which Councillor W.E. Hincks might with advantage cast his eyes upon. The back living-room windows of a number of houses look into the yard adjoining the slaughterhouse. Immediately opposite is a pen, in which a struggling mass of sheep are herded to await slaughter, the poor brutes oft times being packed almost on top of one another. Killing occasionally takes place in the yard itself, just under the house windows, and more than one bullock has been shot there because of its ferocity. The bleating of sheep and the moaning of cattle, previous to their execution, is an intolerable nuisance to the inhabitants of the houses, who put up sheets of newspaper to the windows to shut out the horrible sights.

One of the tenants but mildly described it when she said 'the continued existence of such things was disgraceful'.

Above: South Albion Street opposite St John the Divine in November 1965. (Newarke Houses Museum) Below left: St John's Avenue seen through the archway from Albion Street at the rear of the old Leicester Evening Mail *building. This is now in the middle of Waterloo Way. (Newarke Houses Museum) Below right: Rathbone Place in 1955, looking east towards East Street.*

Above: An inspector from the Council's Health Department holds a measure outside a cottage in a court which was at the rear of Eldon and Upper Hill Streets. The façade of the Trades Hall (now the Swaminarayan Hindu Mission) on St James Street can be seen in the background. The photograph dates from the mid-1930s.

Right: Another view of the same court looking towards Hill Street. In 1815, Hill Street was known as Sandpit Lane, but it was renamed after Dr John Hill, who kept a private lunatic asylum on Belgrave Gate in the early 19th century.

St James Street in the 1930s, just up from the Palais de Danse and opposite the Trades Hall. A health inspector stands close to the narrow entry to Oak Cottages. This was a yard with three houses which were back-to-back with a factory. Today the site is occupied by the Leicester Progressive Spiritualist Church and all that remains are some glazed bricks from the factory entrance.

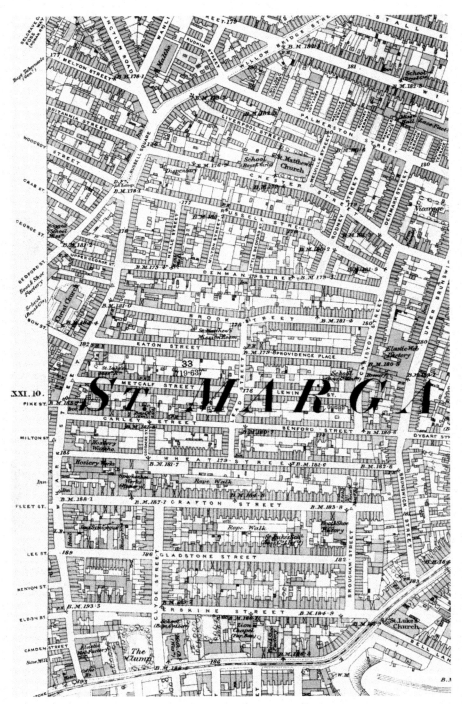

The area to the east of Wharf Street from the 1885 25in Ordnance Survey map.

Above: Wharf Street looking from Humberstone Gate (Newarke Houses Museum).

Below: Wharf Street and Eldon Street in the 1950s. Carr's Fever Powder was originally manufactured by Edwin Carr at No. 168 Wharf Street. (Newarke Houses Museum)

Wharf Street looking towards Humberstone Gate. The junction with Metcalf Street is on the left. (Newarke Houses Museum)

Wharf Street

Leicester Mercury, 3 September 1955.
Wharf Street was a street full of different businesses. In fact, most of the working-class housing in this area was not on Wharf Street itself, but on the many streets like Carley, Metcalf, Eaton and Brook Streets which led from it. These streets were the oldest in the area dating from the 1820s. However, in typical Leicester fashion, this whole area was abbreviated to 'Wharf Street' and used as a generic term to describe Leicester's slum areas. The article below was written as clearance was underway.

I took a stroll around the Wharf Street area yesterday afternoon. What a change is taking place there. The once bustling street where years ago small traders made tidy fortunes is at a standstill compared with what one can recall. In other days it had such a glorious mixture of shops, butchers and poulterers, not forgetting the rabbits, general grocers, greengrocers and all the rest with a liberal sprinkling of pubs. And time was when some people in the sedate parts of Leicester sent to Wharf Street for their best steak and roasting joints, because the butchers there would buy a good beast but the local trade was all for offal and the cheaper cuts. In those days the shopkeepers in Wharf Street did more business on Saturday nights open until 11 o'clock and on Sunday mornings than they did throughout the rest of a week.

Above: Wharf Street, pictured halfway between Humberstone Gate and Russell Square. The Jolly Angler pub is in the distance and the George IV pub is on the right. (Newarke Houses Museum)

Below: Wharf Street at its junction with Bedford Street leading into Russell Square. (Newarke Houses Museum)

Above: Russell Square at its junction with Bedford Street and Woodboy Street in the early 1950s. During the 1918 general election, a hostile audience forced Ramsay MacDonald MP to take shelter in the underground lavatories which are seen above. MacDonald went on to become Labour's first prime minister. Today the lavatories are gone and Russell Square, like St Matthew's estate, is cut off from the city centre by a dual carriageway, and from St Mark's estate by Dysart way. (Newarke Houses Museum).

Russell Square and its Meetings

C. Kirk, The Wyvern, 17 November 1900 (excerpt).

Surely it will be admitted that more speeches have been delivered in Russell Square than on any other spot in the town. Speeches, generally without reason, very loose-pointed and self-contradictory have been made here by the thousand, and the last one has not yet been made. Anti-vaccination and teetotal meetings were once the rage; the Salvation Army speakers in their hurried and fervent appeals have dropped h's on Russell Square when preaching:

'A Refuge to the neighb'ring poor
And strangers led astray.'

Here parliamentary candidates have talked their nonsense and have pleasingly tickled the electoral ear: and after the exciting contest from which we have recently emerged, we all ought to know what nonsense can be scattered by parliamentary candidates.

Russell Square has been the favoured spot of the local Socialist. Here, above all places, the floodgates of his oratory have been opened. On this spot most of the distinguished and many of the extinguished lights of Socialism have paraded their spacious oratory. Indeed, this place has and is a modern Tower of Babel, where speech-making confusion reigns supreme.

As can be seen, Russell Square is not a square at all but an elongated junction. The above view, from the early 1950s, shows the slums of Willow Bridge Street in the background, Junction Road on the left and Chester Street on the right. (Newarke Houses Musem).

Below: Looking from Russell Square towards Humberstone Gate. Russell Street is on the left. (Newarke Houses Museum)

149

Looking down Chester Street towards Russell Square, c.1954. St Matthew's School (opened in 1869) is on the right and St Mark's Church can be seen in the distance. (Newarke Houses Museum)

Stoneygate and Wharf Street

Leicester Pioneer, *25 January 1925 (excerpt).*

The distinguishing features of modern civilised communities is an extreme contrast. Great wealth and extreme poverty; high intellect and deep intellect; supreme art and drab ugliness. Take any civilised city such as Leicester, for instance, and you will find two distinct communities, different in the language they speak, the dress they wear and the houses they live in. To bring it down to the concrete, Stoneygate and Wharf Street.

The denizens of Stoneygate (strange name for such surroundings) would draw their silks lightly about them should they have occasion to explore the black blocks of Wharf Street, and the selfsame inhabitants of these blocks, should they venture so far away from their surroundings as Stoneygate, would look with eyes of wonder, or upturned nose of scorn, at everything that met their gaze. These two classes represent the opposite poles of modern society. The comparison serves to emphasise the fact that society is divided into two great classes – the workers and the idlers; the rich and the poor.

The question that here suggests itself is: why should there be a 'Stoneygate' on the one hand and a 'Wharf Street' on the other? Why should it be possible for only a part of the community to live in the best houses in the city, able to keep staffs of servants to do all the menial work they require, to enjoy the luxury of one or more motor cars to take them where ever they go; to have the benefit of all the best schools, to sit in the best places at the opera and generally monopolise all the advantages which modern science and modern art is supposed to have conferred on humanity as a whole?

Inventive skill has made it possible for boots and shoes of good quality to be produced by the hundred thousand, yet a large proportion of the community, represented by 'Wharf Street', are ill-shod. Clothing, underwear, furniture, bicycles, pianos and all the hundred-and-one necessities of life, as a result of organised industry and modern machinery, are produced practically as easily as water runs from a spring, yet hundreds of thousands, nay millions of people in this country are either without these things altogether or what they do possess of them are either shoddy or second-hand, and most of them are acquired at great sacrifice. Is this diversity of fortune a necessity? Is it a divine or a natural law that there must of necessity be rich and poor; idlers and workers?

Looking from Rodney Street into Russell Street. The Earl Russell pub is situated on the right.

The Warrens of the Poor

F. W. Rogers, Leicester Pioneer, *4 October 1902 (excerpt).*
Wyggeston Ward encompassed Bedford Street and Wharf Street, stretching over to Humberstone Road. The trade directories list ice cream makers in Russell Square, Bedford Street and Wharf Street.

Wyggeston Ward has the unenviable reputation of being the most densely populated ward in the town, there being 143 people to the acre, while Aylestone Ward has only six to the acre. It is true the death-rate is lower than Newton and other wards, but if dirt and malodorous stenches are a criterion, then the ward ought to be the most deadly in the town. Perhaps the people thrive in spite of it.

Wyggeston Ward is the Mecca of the ice cream industry. Here the production of this succulent dainty flourishes with unrivalled vigour. Last week I inspected one or two of these places, and resolutely decided never to touch ices again. Ugh! In the first place visited, the industry was carried on in conjunction with other trades hardly of a kindred nature. The first portion of the establishment was devoted to the sale of various kinds of fish, rabbits, etc., the offal from which distinctly 'hummed'; while the next section was fully equipped for the sale of coal in small quantities of 14lbs and upwards. From here one passes on to what is, or has been, an emporium of rags, bones, rabbit skins, etc., the concentrated effluvia from all these trades blending to give double piquancy to the manufacture of ice cream, which was carried on in the same building. We are told that these places have been visited by the sanitary authorities and have been, like the cottage homes, found to be 'clean and in good order'. Maybe so, but perhaps the inspector does not care for ice cream sandwiches, such as the small child loveth.

Round the corner was another building used for the process of ice cream making and in dangerous proximity to a stable. Yet another, a little further on, was similarly situated; the short, clay-piped gentleman being engaged at the time of my visit in breaking up the ice near the open stable door. All this makes me shudder at the prospect of what may lurk in the innocent 'aporth of ice cream so eagerly devoured by our infantile population. I should like Dr Millard to apply the bacteriological test to a purchase. Methinks he would be able to develop some rare cultures from the experiment.

Mr A. Welton, a sanitary inspector, talking to Mrs E.A. Wye, one of the last remaining residents of Benford Street, in October 1954. (The Leicester Mercury)

Homes of Immorality

This is bad, but there is worse to follow. There are a number of houses in this ward well-known to the Watch Committee as being nothing more or less than brothels. It is an ugly word, but facts are best stated in plain English. What I want to know is this: would these be allowed to continue for seven days if they were situated in Knighton Ward instead of Wyggeston Ward? Yet these places are well-known, the lady occupier having been once before convicted for letting her houses out for such an infamous traffic. The owner of the property in question is also a lady (name and address on application), the house being rented to the second lady for a rent varying from 2s 10p to 5s per week. She, in turn, sub-lets, charging to the poor unfortunates who use them 5s each per room, thus getting 10s rent for a two-roomed house. This is profit. It is perfectly futile to say the authorities have no power to deal with the infamy without well-authenticated facts. As I have suggested, had it been in a better-class neighbourhood it would not have been tolerated for 10 hours. Facts could easily be obtained, sufficient to justify the clearing out of these places, if they were in earnest about it. Parts of this ward are perfect sinks of iniquity. I understand the Watch Committee are going to light the district with incandescent lamps. Is that all? I wager the chairman of the Watch Committee has never been down the district at night more than once in his life. Let some of the committee go down for themselves and see what sort of conditions these people have to exist among.

Above: Brook Street seen from its junction with Lead Street in August 1955. Bill White (father of Ernie) is the lone shopkeeper; the tenants of the street having been moved out sometime earlier. (The Leicester Mercury)

Below: Lead Street at its junction with Metcalf Street. The junction with Carley Street is in the distance. (Newarke Houses Museum)

Above: Lead Street in April 1952. The caption to the photograph reads: 'Lead Street is not an isolated instance of slum conditions in Leicester. Especially in St Margaret's Ward there are too many streets unseen by the majority where families lack amenities which today are considered quite essential.' The picture was taken before the clearance of the Wharf Street area began, so the partially demolished houses must be a result of the closure of individually unfit houses. (The Leicester Mercury).

Right: A backyard in the Wharf Street area.

Right: Hopes Place, Eaton Street. (The Leicester Mercury)

Carley Street Church seen from Goodacre Street in the early 1950s. (Newarke Houses Museum)

This Is The Answer

Councillor Bertram Powell, Illustrated Leicester Chronicle, *1 September 1951*
At the end of the war the Council's immediate priority was to build new houses, rather than to knock down existing ones. However, by the early 1950s the patience of those stuck in slum housing was beginning to wear thin.

With tears streaming down her cheeks, Mrs—— asked me if I could do anything to get her a house. Her story, with slight variations, is typical of hundreds in St Margaret's Ward. Husband and wife and two children living in the tumbledown hovel with 'inlaws', no privacy and not enough space to observe human decency. Crying of children upsetting the temper of the old folk and the consequent bickering and nervous strain, leading in this case to a threatened separation.

It would be difficult to estimate the unhappiness, tension and bad health due to the strained human relationships arising from the housing conditions such as exist in St Margaret's Ward. Apart from the actual insanitary places themselves and the effect on health, the mental torture is grievous. Many of the women in the area in the vicinity of Wharf Street are putting up a valiant fight against the odds to keep themselves and their children clean and respectable. It is pathetic to visit some of the houses to see the unceasing effort to keep paper on the walls, the amateur painting to cover rotten woodwork, the polish to tumbledown grates, the care of steps and floors. The only good thing one can say about the situation is the patience, cheerfulness and effort shown by the people who live there. Without exaggerating, 75 per cent of the houses in the streets like Carley Street are without taps or sinks. Most are without larders. What this means in the hot weather in terms of food pollution is beyond description. Old boxes, home-made cupboards with a piece of cloth in place of a door, are the only places for keeping food. Most of the

Above left: Nos 4–12 Carley Street. Above right: 4–16 Metcalf Street, looking towards Wharf Street. Both pictures date from the early 1950s. These streets ran parallel to each other and were built before 1850. They were demolished to make way for phase one of the St Matthew's estate. Both streets have now disappeared from the map.

'coalhouses' consist of a space under the stairs where dust and dirt fly out into the living room because there is no door. Parlours are a luxury. Privacy is impossible.

In some houses the straw and plaster bedroom floor has broken down and the dirty straw hangs over the dining table like an evil festoon ready to shower dust on the food at the slightest touch. Some lavatories have no water connection and one at least has no door. Many are in an unsafe condition. The same may be said of some chimney stacks. Only the width of one brick separates the people from the weather. These single-brick outer walls are bulging and to the eye of the observer appear to be in danger of collapse. What is to be done?

The St Margaret's Councillors have time and again brought these things to the notice of the City Council, but nothing is done to remove this canker from the city centre.

A Letter

Illustrated Leicester Chronicle, *8 September 1951.*

Sir, I have lived in Carley Street for nearly 50 years, so I think I am qualified to give an opinion about the black spots. Children can be seen any evening sliding down the slates of the lavatories and in general having an orgy of destruction. Of course, it is always other people's property and there is the occasional 'Don't do that you naughty boy' – nothing stronger.

Should the sufferers interfere they run the risk of harm. Any complaint brings: 'You were young once yourself weren't you?' but no action. The doorless lavatory came about like that. First the door was a swing; then (unhinged) a seesaw and, finally, firewood. The wall alongside that particular lavatory took longer to demolish – a year or more – because of shortage of labour.

How can anyone believe new property would remain new without a radical change in the existing control and discipline? I could do with a move from this brick-and-mortar jungle of drunken brawls, unlicensed and half-starved dogs and cats etc. As jungle law is ' Might is right', I must use no name.

OLD 'UN, Carley Street, Leicester

A Co-op milk float in Providence Place. Wharf Street can be seen in the distance. (Newarke Houses Museum)

Below left: Wash houses at the rear of Eaton Street. (Newarke Houses Museum)
Below right: The backyards of Wharf Street in July 1954. (The Leicester Mercury)

Mrs Maude Batchelor in April 1955. She lived at No. 62 Eaton Street and had to carry all her water from a communal tap in the yard. She also did all her washing out in the open in a broken stone sink. She and her husband had applied for a Council bungalow in Humberstone in 1949 but were still waiting. (The Leicester Mercury)

Nos 62–66 Eaton Street in 1954, at its junction with Lead Street.

Charles Keene was one of the most influential local politicians of the 1940s and 1950s. Together with John Beckett, the City Planning Officer, he led the post-war slum clearance programme and wrestled with the problems of redevelopment. The Conservatives suggested that the decisions to build housing on what is now St Matthew's estate would be known as 'Keene's Clanger'. While the population of the estate has changed over the years, it still remains one of the poorer areas of Leicester, which is hardly surprising since it replaced Wharf Street. (The Leicester Mercury)

Slum Clearance

Charles R. Keene, compiled from Leicester Evening Mail *and* Leicester Mercury, *29 October 1952.*
The Leicester Mercury *commented: 'An excellent idea, it will be agreed, but what baffles me is how the Corporation will be able to find the men and material to run a slum clearance scheme alongside the normal housing programme.'*

There appears to be a general recognition that the time has arrived when slum clearance, which has been in abeyance for 13 years, should be resumed. There are 17 different areas in the city, totalling about 4,000 houses in the first period. The greatest concentration of this property lies to the east of Wharf Street. On the grounds of bad housing alone, there is a strong case to deal with the Wellington Street area first. The Health Committee and the Medical Officer of Health would have preferred this area to have been dealt with. It was the subject of compulsory purchase orders before the war. The committee, however, had to have regard to the fact that the site when cleared would be utilised for the central relief road and purposes other than housing. Of the 275 houses originally scheduled in the Wellington Street area, only 143 are now occupied, so the committee was unable to recommend that the site should be cleared immediately. The whole of the Wharf Street area was included in the city development plan as an area for comprehensive development.

The proposals before the Council refer to part of this area, consisting of six acres and containing 272 houses, together with a small number of other types of properties. I do not know whether we will build flats or houses or both on these sites…it is impossible to carry through a scheme in the central areas for anything like the cost that it could be done for on undeveloped land. There will have to be the greatest skill in planning the site and buildings if it is to be developed economically. The extent to which the Housing Committee can make available new dwellings is one of the most important considerations in determining the cope of our work. It will take many years to complete and will require the collaboration of all the chief officers and departments of the City Council.

Providence Place, looking from Eaton Street towards Christow Street. These houses had common yards and outside toilets. The factory at the end of the street is the Boston Blacking Company, which was the precursor of Bostik. (Author)

The headline from the Leicester Mercury, 7 January 1953. After a halt of 14 years occasioned by the war and its legacy, the Council announced plans to restart slum clearance. Government approval for the demolition of the 349 houses in the Lewin clearance area was granted the following year. The headline was slightly misleading in that there were no back-to-back houses in the Lewin Street area. (The Leicester Mercury)

For Mrs. J. Pryor, of 26, Providence Place, Leicester, wash-day is a backyard operation—the house is too small. These houses will disappear under the Lewin Street clearance scheme.

LEICESTER TO MAKE A START ON SLUM CLEARANCE

Most Of Back-To-Back Houses Will Disappear

Above: Typical court houses in Russell Street in the early 1950s.

Below: A view of Russell Street looking towards the Braziers Arms in Russell Square. The TV aerials suggest that this picture dates from the 1950s. (Author)

The Palmerstone Street area from the 1885 25in Ordnance Survey map.

Looking down Curzon Street from its junction with Taylor Street in 1961. The poster on the right advertises good secure jobs in the mines for men and boys. (Leicester City Council)

A Memorial from 29 Inhabitants of the Curzon Street Area

Minutes of the Highways and Sewage Committee, 31 August 1853.
The origin of the Humberstone Road estate of the Freehold Land Society lay in an attempt by local radicals to give working men the vote in Parliamentary elections. This is reflected in streets, like Cobden and Bright, being named after Liberal politicians. After 1832, the standard qualification for a vote was the ownership of a house with an annual rental value of 40 shillings. The Freehold Land Society was founded in 1849 with the radical John Biggs as its chairman. It bought land at wholesale prices and then subdivided it into 40-shilling plots. Membership was by subscription and plots were allocated by a lucky draw.

The society aimed to lay out its estates so as to make the streets as 'airy, healthful and respectable' as possible and was responsible for about a fifth of Leicester's housing built during 1851 and 1881. Unfortunately, the society did not put any restrictions on the use of plots taken up by its members, many of whom could not afford to build a house for themselves. Plots were often sold on to builders and landlords who then crammed as many houses on to the site as possible by building rows of cottages in back garden spaces. The following is a letter of protest to the Council against the development proposed by the builder Thomas Bland, which the Council was unable to oppose.

Gentlemen, we find that foundations have now been laid for several miserable hovels in the background, and that the number of houses will be as great and the plan upon which they are to be built tenfold more objectionable than we at first supposed possible. The plans upon which these houses are being built is filthy and sets common decency at defiance; the houses have only one door and that in front, so that all the filth, dung, refuse etc. that is made in each house must be brought out in the presence of all the neighbourhood and taken to a cluster of public privies, to be built close to the front door in front of the houses, or it must remain in the house breeding fever and malaria on a scale never surpassed in the most

163

A composite photograph of Russell Square (left) and Junction Road as seen from Willow Bridge Street, c.1960. (Leicester City Council)

horrible dens that London or Liverpool contained in the days when sanitary boards had no existence and avaricious men were allowed to prejudice the public health and degrade the poor to their hearts' content. We have no hesitation in saying that houses such as these are unfit for human inhabitation and are calculated to debase the minds and habits of those whose poverty may drive them to seek shelter in such dens.

Palmerstone Street

Tom Barclay, The Wyvern, 7 June 1895.
Not long after this article was published, Argyle Cottages and one side of Melville Terrace were knocked down in one of the few pieces of 19th-century slum clearance. The land was turned into a children's playground (in the 1920s there were only four such playgrounds in Leicester). Palmerston Street soon after disappeared from maps and became an extension of Taylor Street from which it led. In 1932 a new school, originally designed as a factory, opened on the site of the remaining terraces off Taylor Street. Today, Vancouver Road follows part of the line where Taylor Street used to be and, at the time of writing, the rest goes through the playground of the school. Present-day Taylor Road is at right angles to the old Taylor Street, while Calgary Road now follows the line of the old Willow Bridge Street.

Walking from Russell Square down (or up) Willow Bridge Street towards what used to be the 'Willow Brig',[1] you come upon Palmerstone Street at the right, not more than 200 yards from the Bedford Street of our last. Palmerstone Street was 30 years ago a rope-walk – Browett's rope-walk – and at that rope-walk a poor, half-starved, ragged, ignorant, awkward, shy, slum-dwelling lad turned the wheel.[2] He was nine years of age, and he worked from 6am to 8pm five days a week, and from 6am to 4pm on Saturdays; that is to say, 68 hours a week. For how much do you think? About one farthing an hour, friends! The fear of being late of a morning so haunted him that he often started up out of sleep, half dressed himself, and went into the street to get to know the time. Finding it only two or three o'clock, he would go to bed again. There was no clock in the house. He next woke, or was called, at perhaps a quarter past six. Then there was dismal crying, from fear of a scolding and cuffing

1. Presumably the bridge across the Willow Brook. The crossing was built in the 1880s to provide additional access to the manure wharf on the Great Northern Railways sidings for the Council's night soil department.
2. A rope-walk was a long, thin area of land used in the manufacture of rope. Hemp fibres were tied to a hook attached to a wheel which was slowly turned while the rope maker walked back down the rope walk, feeding out additional fibres from the supply he carried.

Looking down Willow Bridge Street towards Russell Square. The entrance to Rudkin Street is on the right, just beyond the children sitting on the pavement reading. (Newarke Houses Museum)

from the 'gaffer', and jeers from the rest. How was he likely to be refreshed by sleep in that stifling little crib of a room where seven slept together, father, mother, two girls and three boys? The bed was a mere shake down of straw on a hard earthen floor. His breakfast was bread and treacle that gave him heartburn; fruit and good vegetables he never knew. A sheep's head, 'tongue-root' or 'eye-piece' of a pig's head was the only meat he ever tasted.

His work hours were excessive and horribly monotonous. He still recalls how the one wish between mealtimes (so-called) was that the dreary, weary hours would come to an end. He was weak, so weak! No sprightliness nor vigour in his little body, so that he often woke as tired as when he lay down to sleep and was slow and stupid and unable to move as quick as he wanted to do. He wonders if there are any poor little wretches like that today, passing through similar experiences.

To return to Palmerstone Street, I may inform you that we have, on the left side from Willow Bridge Street, six or seven 'terraces', as they are pompously called, with 14 houses in each terrace. Both front and back yards are pretty wide, I will say that; but whether it is that the houses were built of bad material, or that they have been 'knocked about', the brick-work is frittering and crumbling and looks most dingy. There is no solidity, no finish about the buildings. You will understand that we belong to that 'other half' of the world about whose ways of living 'one half', the half up Stoneygate and Highfields, know so little. We are scissors-grinders, glaziers and 'mush-fakers', and our women stitch gloves at starvation wages. Of course, there are tackers and finishers among us. In Granville Terrace there are 10 houses to let out of 14, but Denmark Terrace is considerably better. In Rodney Terrace we have three of the houses turned into 'The Palmerstone Street Mission', and a board announces Sunday religious services and weekday gospel temperance services. The public house across the way announces on a card in the window that ale brewed from malt and hops is there sold for 3d a quart. In Melville Terrace again, there are nine houses to let, and Palmerstone Terrrace is little better, but Willow Brook Cottages are all tenanted; although the rents are 6d higher.

The fact is, lots of us like a neat-looking and well-built house just as much as middle-class people. We take pleasure in our homes and like to see them clean, and you cannot

The junction of Taylor Street and Stanley Street looking towards the George and Dragon pub, c.1960. Stanley Street was demolished after 1961. (Leicester City Council)

keep a badly-built house very clean. When the houses in these terraces began to want repairing, I am told the tenants notified the same respectfully to the agent who collected the rents, but that the agent put off repairs from week to week, pooh-poohed complaints and misrepresented things to the owners of the property. I am told again that the property owners left things entirely in the hands of the agent. Diamond began to cut diamond; the owners could not repair and the tenants would not pay rent. Some managed to stay three months without paying any; others went away in debt and actually came back to the same house after some weeks. Cupboards have been used for fire-lighting, windows are broken right and left. I should say there are windows in every court crippled – brown paper plastered over them like a bandage on a drunkard's broken head. In one instance, the window has been taken clean out by somebody. Altogether a sorry rather dilapidated lot of houses; but there are at the moment I write, whitewashers, paperhangers, carpenters and other renovators busy on them. As rents go the houses are not dear if only inhabitable. Three shillings for a four-roomed house centrally situated cannot be said to be exorbitant. I thought I would like to know what the intellectual recreations of the inhabitants of these regions were like, so I walked into a hostelry in the immediate vicinity and ordered a horehound[3] beer; and as I sat imbibing the same I was edified by the following deeply reasoned philosophical discussion:

'Do you remember when Bendigo won the Derby?'

'Do I remember; (with a scornful emphasis on the do, as who should say do you imagine I could be so ignorant) don't I.'

'Well, who rode the winner?'

'Why, Glover rode the winner.'

'He did not.'

'Didn't he? I know he did.'

---

3. A very bitter herb used to flavour beer.

The Willow Bridge Inn on the junction of Syston Street and Willow Bridge Road, c. 1960. (Leicester City Council)

'What'll ye bet on it?'

'I've got nowt now, but you'll find my words true.'

'We then, I tell you Osborne rode Bendigo, that's who rode Bendigo, and don't you forget it.'

'I ain't likely to forget it. I think I know what I'm talking about; I was there.'

'Ah, and so was I; I won a bit o' money that day.'

'And didn't I? I know I did. And I didn't see the race neither. I'd got my eyes fixed on a bookme'ker all the while – didn't mean him to sling it,' (i.e., to abscond) 'not till he paid me.'

'Well but your wrong about etc., etc.'

'I tell you I'm not; it was etc etc.' Ad nauseam, ad absurdum, ad infinitum.

These men surely believe neither in a future life nor in the dignity and sacredness of this. There exist no social problems for them. They look for no progress. They are dead to all that we mean by culture, and little removed from Carlyle's self-satisfied animal with plenty of 'hog-wash'.

But there are all sorts and conditions in our class as in other classes, and no criticism is worth a rush that takes the first two or three individuals it comes across and concludes that they are specimens of a whole neighbourhood. Here, for instance, is a brave, patient, struggling widower left with a family of small children, who is sober as the goddess of health herself, devoting every farthing of his scanty wages to bringing up his little ones decently. His eldest daughter, by the death of the mother, is at 16 already turned into a housewife, with all the cares of stitching, washing, scrubbing, cooking, nursing and general management of a household. Here is another chap, honest as daylight, free as rain, a regular worker, and a reader of books and papers on political and social questions; and if he does have a few glasses of beer on a Saturday night, he is quiet and sensible with them, and 'All' us looks ater the missis and the nippers first. There's Thrifty Ted, too, who buys his potatoes and flour and other goods wholesale, so

The Curzon Arms, on the junction of Taylor Street and Curzon Street, had a bar which measured only 13ft long by 6ft 6in wide. The newly built blocks of St Matthew's phase one on Russell Square can be seen in the distance beyond Taylor Street School on the right. (Leicester City Council)

as 'to make a bit'. He doesn't mean, he says, when he's done up at the factory, to have to go to the 'Bassy', i.e. Bastile.[4]

Next door to him is Jack Townsend, one of the unemployed, who has had to pawn all the best 'togs' of the family and sell some of the furniture in order to carry on. His girls will not go to the chapel again till they can get their 'things' out, and Jack looks gloomy and desperate, though his wife tries to comfort him. 'What's the matter, Dad?' asks the youngest of his children while I am on a visit. 'Are you in trouble?' Dad smiles sarcastically and answers, 'Ay, I am my duck – going off my head because I haven't a chance to work 12 hours a day – for somebody else'. Jack has come under the influence of the Socialists and by 'somebody else' he means the Capitalists.

Here is Fred Colton who has no regular trade, and works at odd jobs such as loading and unloading for brokers and auctioneers. Some times he goes water-cressing, and the family being bad off for beds, he actually sleeps on a sack spread over the damp watercress. His mother never undresses for weeks and sleeps in a box. The poor woman has got dipsomania. She is wretched until her gloves are stitched. Soon as she can draw the money for them, off she waddles to the 'long pull' with a bottle. She knows her husband will beat her for drinking, but drink she will. She does not 'nip' and then take peppermint or lozenges to sweeten the breath, like craftier and more moderate dames. No! She must muddle herself with the first money she clutches. Drink is her all – her god. It is as though her miserable conditions goaded her to drink and drug herself into oblivion, while the drinking creates the miserable conditions to a great extent. Miserable woman truly! Whose husband absents himself from home as much as possible; whose daughters will not entrust her with their earnings, though they take her part when the father wants to thrash her; whose son has no respect for her, and calls her atrocious names, although she dotes on him. He drinks, too, though he hates to see his mother

---

4. Bassy or Bastile: the workhouse (an allusion to the French Bastille).

The Wanlip Inn on the junction of Wanlip Street and Lower Willow Street. These streets were demolished sometime after 1960. (Leicester City Council)

have any. It makes him furious to find the bottle about and he goes off slamming doors and using vile names; whereupon the wretched mother goes in a flood of tears complaining to the neighbours. Her husband's blows and her daughters' reproaches affect her very little, but when 'our Fred' loses his temper and 'gets on to her' like that it breaks his mother's heart. This is the touch of nature that makes her kin to us. The neighbour women then look meaningly, sympathetically, at one another; they light her fire for her, make her tea, get her to sleep, tell the son the first time they see him that he ought to be ashamed of himself, and beg of the husband as he is coming home from work to 'let her off this time'.

The foregoing is a very sad, and I hope a very exceptional, case. Do not let me give your readers the impression that it is connected with Palmerstone Street; I have not said so. Generally the case is reversed: it is the husband who bullies, starves, robs and ruins his family, the grey mare being decidedly the best horse, who manages to pull her family through, when her yoke-fellow refuses to pull with her.

Life In the Slums

T.M. Robinson, The Wyvern, 23 June 1899 (excerpt).
Robinson lived in Brunswick Terrace off Taylor Street. Brunswick Terrace eventually became part of the site of Taylor Road School.

Those who only enter the slums when on business see very little of what takes place almost daily, or are aware of the extreme poverty and suffering many endure. They are equally ignorant also as to the destructiveness and audacity of the children. These little folks appear to think they have as much right to enter a neighbour's house as their own, and what is more they will not be turned out if they can help it. If you send one out at the front door, in another minute he will enter by the back. Send him out again, and

Syston Street was typical of the long monotonous terraces built after the 1859 bye-laws. This view looks towards Willow Bridge Street and Brunswick Street past the Midlands Clubs brewery on the left. Syston Street was demolished after 1962 and the street is now cut in two by St Mark's estate. (Leicester City Council)

then he will climb on the window sill if he cannot get into the house. He will make grimaces and cover the window with dirty, greasy finger marks. The following occurred recently.

A little fellow about five years old entered a neighbour's house about 11am, the other Sunday. Breakfast was then on the table, so the lad laid down on the hearth-rug and lolled about. He had nothing on but a shirt, which was filthy. One of the family left the table and immediately the boy took his place, helped himself to the half cup of tea and bread and butter, then got down and went home.

Some slum children are not shy, they do not wait for an invitation, but generally help themselves to anything on the table if there is an opportunity. You can see them running about on Sundays at noon neither washed nor dressed. They are allowed to remain up until their parents retire to bed, which on Saturdays is often after midnight. On Sundays, too, you may see them sitting out in groups in the yards at about 11pm. These are children whose ages range from a few months to 12 or 14 years. During the day they amuse themselves at every game they can think of, often forcing up the stones in the yards to play 'duck'. Whenever a house becomes untenanted the windows soon get broken and an entrance is gained this way if the doors happen to be secured. Even the latter are soon smashed. But all slum children are not so wantonly destructive. Occasionally you will come across one who knows his manners and will not associate with the others in mischief, but these are very scarce indeed. One scarcely knows what to think of parents whose children are seldom (if ever) corrected when seen doing wrong. The other day a lad of about 14 was playing pitch and toss in front of his own home and the boy's parents were within. He confessed that he won a shilling on Saturday afternoon. In these large yards the police cannot see what goes on, and have no access except through one of the houses. Youths and young men know this, so sit gambling for hours undisturbed.

Melton Street (to the right) and Junction Road looking towards Belgrave Gate (Leicester City Council)

Above: Cranbourne Street was built in the 1870s and ran between Catherine Street and Belgrave Road. It is now the site of the Sainsburys store. The large factory is the C.W.S.

works on the south side of Cranbourne Street, which was built for the former Leicester Co-operative Hosiery Manufacturing Society. These pictures were taken in 1969. (Newarke Houses Museum)

Left: Spinner Street, which ran between Taylor Street and Willow Street. (Leicester Mercury)

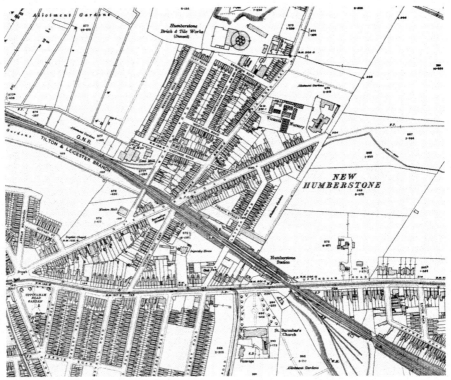

The rural surroundings of New Humberstone from the 1915 Ordnance Survey map.

New Humberstone

Tom Barclay, The Wyvern, 14 June 1895.
During the course of his life Tom Barclay moved fairly frequently. At the time this article was
written he was living at No. 22 Eastbourne Road in New Humberstone. The previous winter,
Barclay had been unemployed for weeks and was reduced to hawking hot peas round the local
pubs (he wrote this up as Some Experiences of a Literary Hot Pea Vendor, alias Pea-bloke). *The*
276 houses in the Morton Road area were demolished after 1967 to make way for a new
Council estate. A new layout meant that some of the streets mentioned below have disappeared.

To the left of the Uppingham Road and not three-quarters of a mile from Old Humberstone is
New Humberstone. Though flat as a pancake, it is salubrious, having a sandy soil, and doctors
have ordered rheumatic and phthisic patients to live there. We are not all slums; on Victoria
Road and elsewhere there are an 'aristocracy of labour' and a fledgling villadom, and Eastbourne
Road is quiet and plodding; but Dover Road and Morton Road have got a bad name, and if, as
great philosophers have averred, poverty is the greatest of crimes and the poor 'bad in the lump',
then a lot of us want improving off the face of the earth. New Humberstone has been a city of
refuge to us when forced to flee from the wrath of the landlords of Leicester; and yet some parts
look as though belonging to a city of the dead.

I venture to say there are no other streets in Leicester and its suburbs where you see so dismal
a sight as in Morton and Dover Roads. In Morton Road are 27 houses 'hand-running' all shut

A long entry off Evans Street in Belgrave, 1960. (Newarke Houses Museum)

up, and have been now for nearly three years. Window openings are mostly boarded up, the fanlights are broken, the windows (when any are left unbroken) are only semi-transparent with dust, and the thresholds and jambs are glutted with dirt. Entry doors are all fastened, but where there is a grille you can see the backyard stones covered with rank grass. In some cases, all doors are open save the front, and you can step in through the window frame on to the brick-end and broken bottle-covered floor. Remnants of old bills are on the walls, offering a £1 reward to anyone informing of wilful damage to the property.

In Dover Road there are 11 houses to let one side and 15 on the other, and these are nearly all next door to one another. There are among these, five-roomed houses at 2/6, six-roomed at 3/- and for 3/6 you can have a six-roomed house with a yard to yourself. The term 'slum' is indeed hardly applicable to these streets, the houses are so large. It is the people who are poor, not the houses. Unquestionably the people are poor; big house and little in it is the order of the day. We put a thick curtain up to the window of the front room (or a piece of stuff if we have no curtain), because we do not want everybody to see there is nothing in it. We have got no shutters, or we would put them too. When the wife goes shopping she brings back the articles under her apron, so that Mrs Smith will not 'gas' about it to Mrs Brown and Mrs Jones. We know one another to be poor, yet when we are having a glass or two together in The Granby, on Saturdays, do we ever admit it? Not we. Even though we had 'pig's butter' for breakfast that morning, we pretend it was bacon and tomatoes we had. Sometimes the following conversation takes place at dinner hour:

HE: 'Haven't ye got any dinner?'

SHE: 'Nothing, only what ye see.*

HE; No 'taters! you might a got a few 'taters.'

SHE: 'I might if I'd got the money; I can't coin it. I haven't a farthing in the house but 3d, and I want soap and blue for the wash, and ——.'

HE: 'Well, 'taters are just as cheap as bread. I'm sick o' bread.'

SHE: 'Ah, and so am I, but I have to put up with it. You can't have 'taters for breakfast, can you? And, besides, what's the girl got to take with her to work? I do all I can, I'm sure; – you know what you gave me, and I had this week the ——.'

Of course we drink a little. We have a beerhouse, The Great Northern, a big hotel called The Granby (in which is a large room partitioned off from the counter into horse boxes), and two or three long pulls. At one 'long pull' on Sunday, at opening time, there is quite a crowd both of children and grown-ups, with every variety of vessel. You have to take your turn and may be 10 minutes waiting. You see, we get nearly a pint for half a pint at the long pull. It does not matter if it is inferior, for to us all beer is good, though some is better! It costs some of us a bit in the year for trams and brakes, so rent stands to need to be cheap.

173

The junction of Checketts Road, Belgrave, with Little Avenue. (Newarke Houses Museum) Below: The junction with Evans Street, c.1960. (Newarke Houses Museum)

The junction of Checketts Road, Belgrave, with Little Avenue, c.1960. (Newarke Houses Museum) Below: Children playing draughts in Clarke Street, Belgrave, c.1960. These streets were demolished sometime after 1970.

Above: The junction of Coventry Street and Dane Street, which runs parallel to King Richard's Road. (Newarke Houses Museum). Below: The junction of New Parks Street and Andrews Street. (Newarke Houses Museum) Coventry Street has now been truncated as a result of the Council's housing development in the Norfolk Street area during the early 1970s.

Above: Great Holme Street at its junction with new Parks Street in 1971. Great Holme Street was demolished to make way for the dual carriageway connecting the Narborough Road with King Richard's Road. (Newarke Houses Museum)

Below: Little Holme Street, which ran as a dog-leg between Leamington Street and New Parks Street. (Newarke Houses Museum)

Baker Street led off St George's Street and was demolished c.1957. The cleared site became home to the Leicester Mercury *building and St George's Way. The cellars of these houses are still believed to exist underneath the present* Mercury *building.*

Constitution Hill from Swain Street bridge. The 30 houses in the Queen Street and St George's Street clearance areas were demolished after 1962.

Casey's Court

Mrs S. Tacey, Illustrated Leicester Chronicle, *1 September 1951.*

I was grieved to read of Leicester's black spot, St Margaret's Ward, but it is not the only black spot. Take a trip to Wycliffe Ward, Baker Street, for instance, which has one tap between six housewives; it is just like Casey's Court on washday especially, all queuing for water. The tap we have takes quite five minutes to fill a bucket. That is not the only pest either, there are cockroaches and mice. There seems nothing we can do about it. People in rooms are better off than we are in so-called houses. They have toilets to themselves and indoor sanitation in most cases.

Before they start making Leicester beautiful they want to make us decent houses to live in, where our children can live a clean, healthy life. It seems we have to have a house full of children before there is any chance of getting a new house. We have only one boy, aged six.

Constitution Hill looking towards Queen Street.

He wants a knife for Christmas to stab the beetles, that is the only idea the children get around here.

All our savings go on decorating, trying to make the place habitable. Every time we decorate, we have to get a plasterer in and pay for it ourselves. In our row of six houses, there is not one child that has not had some serious illness. We have always got the doctor at one of the houses. My husband is a disabled soldier. Is this the best that can be done for him after six years of fighting?

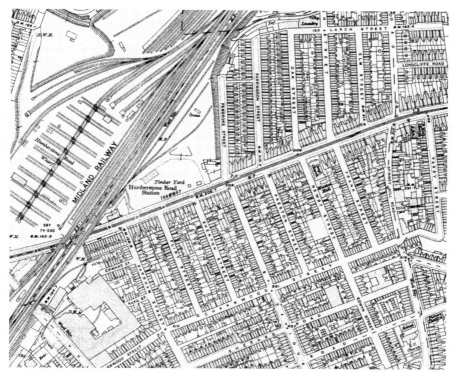

The Charnwood Street area from the 1913 Ordnance Survey map. The houses in the Larch Street area, to the north of Humberstone Road, were not demolished until after 1974.

Charnwood Street

In the 1950s, Charnwood Street was what Bedford Street had been 50 years before. Known locally as 'Charny', it had over 100 small shops and was the nearest thing that Leicester had to Petticoat Lane. Charnwood Street itself was a shopping street rather than a street of unfit housing and its demolition was a by-product of the clearance process. It was a demolition which was regretted soon after and its loss contributed to the Council's later commitment to urban renewal.

The houses in the area were built between 1870–80 and a public enquiry into their proposed clearance was held in 1968. The Council argued that the houses were unfit, badly arranged, at the end of their useful life and based on an 'obsolete street pattern'. The Council's intention was to redevelop the area for residential use with provision for a shopping centre and for four primary schools to replace the existing obsolete one. However, in order to facilitate this redevelopment a number of perfectly fit houses also had to be demolished.

The residents of the many unfit houses in Preston Road, Flint Street and the other nearby terraces were no doubt pleased to be rehoused and the new Charnwood estate provided a better standard of housing. However, the loss of a shopping street where one could buy staple needs at rock-bottom prices was keenly felt. The comprehensive redevelopment of the area had failed to provide what people actually wanted and voices were soon questioning whether wholesale clearance was still the answer.

179

Charnwood Street in May 1957. The Leicester Mercury *wrote that 'Charnwood Street is probably the most unexpected in Leicester. After rows of quiet residential streets, still nursing a Victorian detachment, you come upon this business thoroughfare which shows that from a commercial and social point of view, it can keep pace with modern urban life.'*

'The shops, as busy during the week and as at weekends, give the street an air of well ordered ease. Goods are displayed outside the windows, as well as inside, enabling shoppers to make their purchases at leisure and at the same time offering them a wide variety. Here is a self-contained community where one would least expect to find it and which has its own friendly "neighbourhood" atmosphere.'

Below: Charnwood Street at its junction with Mere Road. This junction and road no longer exists. Ivan Slack was one of the many dealers on Charnwood Street.

Above: Charnwood Street in June 1962 when it was described by the Leicester Mercury *as 'a thoroughfare unrivaled anywhere in Leicester, out of the town centre, for its diversity of trade. And there's still a deal of second-hand bargaining too.'* (The Leicester Mercury). *Below: Another view of Charnwood Street not long before its demolition.*

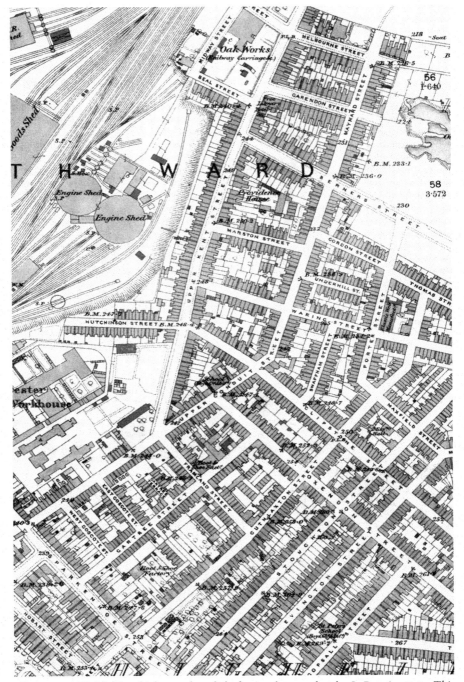

The area of Highfields which was demolished to make way for the St Peter's estate. This is taken from the 1885 25in Ordnance Survey map.

Hutchison Street, looking across Upper Kent Street to Clipstone Street in 1965. (Newarke Houses Museum)

The junction of Upper Conduit Street and West Goscote Street in 1965. (Newarke Houses Museum)

Cox's newsagents on Clipstone Street was situated next to a business which repaired umbrellas. (Newarke Houses Museum)

Nos 51–58 Conduit Street from Upper Fox Street, 1965. (Newarke Houses Museum)

Guthlaxton Street in 1965. It was one of the few street names which survived the building of the St Peter's estate. Guthlaxton Street achieved a degree of notoriety during the riots in the early 1980s as Leicester's 'front line'. (Newarke Houses Museum)

The junction of Conduit Street and Sparkenhoe Street in 1965, now the site of the Leicester Central Mosque. (Newarke Houses Museum)

The north-east side of Gordon Street (Nos 2–34) in 1965. The view is taken from Porter Street looking towards Upper Conduit Street. (Newarke Houses Museum)

Thomas Street in 1965, looking towards Melbourne Road. The large shadow is cast by Briggs' Tannery. Thomas Street ran parallel to Berners Street. (Newarke Houses Museum)

Waring Street looking from the junction with Upper Conduit Street towards Briggs' Tannery and St Paul's Church on Melbourne Road and Dale Street. (Newarke Houses Museum)

Cramant Cottages in 2009, 51 years after they were scheduled for demolition. Now restored, this row of cottages houses a pre-school nursery. The small rooms make excellent play spaces for the children and the courtyard is covered by an atrium.

Bartholomew Street in 2009, 35 years after it was scheduled for demolition. In 1968, the 165 houses in Bartholomew and Biddulph Streets were designated as part of an improvement area. In 1974, the Council changed its mind and decided to clear the area instead. The local residents' association and Shelter argued that these houses should not be demolished and could have a useful life once they were improved. Their determined campaign saved the houses from the bulldozer and these streets became one of the first local housing action areas. Seen above are local residents Mike Pepper (left) and Andrew Legg (right), who were active in the campaign and were assisted by their then Councillors Jim Wintour and Peter Soulsby (centre).

Above and below: Undated photographs of Tom Barclay. The one above was taken by his friend and fellow Socialist Archibald Gorrie.

Tom Barclay was born in Leicester in 1852, a child of Irish Catholic immigrants, and grew up in the heart of the town's slum districts. Because they were written from the perspective of an inhabitant, his descriptions of life in Leicester's slums are unique.

During the 1890s, Barclay was a frequent contributor to the topical weekly magazine *The Wyvern*. As well as the articles on Leicester's slums, which are reproduced here, he wrote on a number of subjects ranging from art criticism to Leicester slang. His contributions were often the winning entries to a weekly competition with a prize of 5/-. At the time, he was working as a house-to-house bill distributor and was a frequent visitor to all the slum districts.

Barclay sometimes wrote under the pseudonyms of 'Armer Teufel' (German for poor devil) and 'Éireannach' (Gaelic for an Irishman or person of Irish descent). He later wrote the story of his life in *Memoirs and Medleys, The Autobiography of a Bottle Washer*, which was published after his death in 1933.

Barclay never went to day school and was taught to read by his mother. At the age of eight he went to work at Browett's rope-walk, where Taylor Street now stands. Later, he worked at Colton's rope-walk where Corah's hosiery factory was situated. He also worked in the shoe trade and then the hosiery trade as a rotary hand's helper. Reading was his great joy and in the 1870s he attended classes at the Working Men's College under the Revd D.J. Vaughan while working at Corah's factory. Here he was taught and influenced by George Newell, a hosiery union leader and Christian Socialist, who become the manager of the Hosiery Co-operative Manufacturing Society. While at college he took certificates in English language, botany, physiography, political philosophy and first aid.

Barclay eventually rejected Catholicism and became a Secularist, influenced by the radical politician Charles Bradlaugh and the writings of the American Robert Ingersoll. Following William Morris's lecture in Leicester on 'Art and Socialism' to the Secular Society, Barclay founded the Leicester branch of the Socialist League in 1885. Barclay became a contributor to Morris's paper *Commonweal* and became the League's chief local lecturer and propagandist, speaking at open-air meetings and lecturing in clubs. Barclay can be seen as the founding father of Socialism in Leicester. Despite Bradlaugh's rejection of Socialism, he remained one of Barclay's heroes. At the news of Bradlaugh's death Barclay was found in St Saviours Road, crying. In 1886, Barclay was briefly general secretary of the Leicester Area Hosiery Union.

Though Barclay loved ideas and debate, he was not a politician. The search for knowledge, books and literature were his loves. He knew Bernard Shaw, Edward Carpenter and corresponded with Ruskin. In the 1880s, Barclay produced a pamphlet that put Ruskin's ideas into a popular format and which went through several editions. In 1885, he produced a weekly newspaper, the *Countryman,* which was distributed free to over 50 villages. It was financed through advertising and the patronage of J.W. Barrs, the Secularist tea merchant.

During his life he was a member of all the early Socialist groups, but he disliked their Sectarianism. In 1892, he set up the *Leicester Pioneer* as a weekly Socialist newspaper, which claimed a readership of 5,000. Barclay was also active in the formation of the Labour Club in Leicester, which later gave rise to the local Independent Labour Party. In 1902 he set up a short-lived branch of the Gaelic League.

Despite the hard conditions of his life, he refused offers of financial help from his friends. The privations of Barclay's childhood had left a deep mark. Although disappointed in love in his teens, when it became clear to him that he would always be poor, he determined never to marry and inflict poverty on his children. Barclay had a wide circle of friends, and his fund of knowledge on books and authors, of humorous tales, of limericks and schoolboy howlers made him excellent company.

He said that over a period of 50 years he had worked in some 20 factories. During the last 25 years of his life his work was mainly that of a bottle washer and as a dyer's labourer. Throughout his life he had an insatiable thirst for knowledge and was a true working-class intellectual and freethinker. It was an abiding trial to him that so many ordinary people took no interest in books, politics, economics, social questions, music or any form of art, but were wholly engrossed in sport, gambling and drink. His obituary observed that 'many of the older generation of Leicester politicians and students will mourn the passing of Tom Barclay...he was in humble circumstances all his life, yet he had more influence on the city's intellectual life than most of those in high stations.' (*Leicester Mercury,* 2 January 1933)

'An Original'

This portrait of Tom Barclay appeared in The Wyvern *of 25 January 1895.*

I cannot say that I have seen this 'admirable Crichton' selling hot peas in public houses, but I have watched him hawking nougat and other toothsome confections, and I know that he can dance a hornpipe and sing a comic song. He is also a first-rate botanist, and it is a liberal education to be his companion on a country walk. In his habits he is a thorough Bohemian, and I am sure he would give the shirt off his back to any poor beggar who carried less spondulicks than himself.

Some years ago he was chief contributor to an ultra radical organ, and in that capacity he wrote leading articles, critiques, reports, verses (grave and gay) and short stories, besides sweeping the office, canvassing for advertisements and carrying copies to newsagents and subscribers in a wheelbarrow. He is never so happy as when he is making economic problems clear to the comprehension of a costermonger in a Leicester court or alley. He is the Socrates of the marketplace and street corner. Although regarded by so-called respectable people, to whom he is a bête noir, as a social pariah, he has corresponded with Stepniak, Prince Kropotkin and William Morris and he has likewise had the honour of dedicating a brochure to John Ruskin, that eminent author, expressing his great pleasure with the same.

The list below is of all the slum clearance areas in Leicester. Each was given a number which is shown on the left of the column. Several streets could be included in one clearance area which for reasons of space cannot be listed below. The dates with * mark the date of City Council approval for a scheme and all other dates are those of Ministry approval. Generally, demolition could follow soon after, though sometimes property could be left standing for some time. The numbers in brackets indicate the number of buildings in the clearance area, which generally approximates the number of houses demolished. War interrupted some pre-war schemes and some unfit housing in the 1970s was improved rather than cleared. These clearance areas do not include individual unfit houses which were demolished.

1–3	Green and Sandacre Streets (238)	1932
4–7	Harvey, Bakehouse, Thornton Lanes, Redcross Street (97)	1935
8,11–15	Britannia, Fleet and Upper Hill Streets (164)	1936
9–10	St Mark's, George and Grove Streets (196)	1935*
17–19	Burley's Lane, Gravel and Abbey Streets (47)	1935*
20–33	Wharf and Bedford Streets, Belgrave (413)	1936
34–42	Burley's and Archdeacon Lanes (245)	1936
43–47	Bath Street and Bonners Lane (72)	1936
48–49	Thornton Lane and Northgate Street (27)	1936*
50–51	Palmer Street (23)	c.1937
52–54	Navigation and Lower Brown Streets (412)	c.1937
55–56	Brierley and Willow Streets (16)	1936*
65	Sanvey Gate (3) demolished after 1954	1937*

67	Causeway Lane (245) demolished after 1954	1937*
79	Great Central Street (368)	1939
80–82	Old Mill Lane and Craven Street (208)	c.1938
83–88	Pasture Lane and Birstall Street (296)	c.1938
89	Wellington Street (272) demolished after 1954	1938
96	Dunkirk Street demolished after 1954	1938
97	Eldon Street (6) demolished after 1954	1938
111	Lewin Street (249)	1954
112	Brunswick Street (7)	1954
114	Metcalf Street (269)	1954
115–19	Russell, Christow, Dysart and Wharf Streets, (675)	1955
120–22	Duke Street etc (78)	1956
123	York Road (18)	1956
124	Friar Lane (21)	1956
125	Baker Street etc. (152)	1956
126	Constitution Hill (26)	1956
127	North Bridge Place (23)	1956
128	Crane Street (30)	1956
129	Friars Causeway (4)	1956
130	Blake Street (2)	1956
131	Foxon Street (34)	1956
132	Royal East Street (8)	1956
133	Orchard Street (3)	1956
134	Pentonville (35)	1956
135	Warrington Street (178)	1956
136	Allan Street (7)	1957
137	St Bernard Street (6)	1957
138	Littleton Street (4)	1957
139	Free Lane (7)	1957
140	Albany Cotts, All Saints Road (16)	1957
141	Woodgate Cotts, Woodgate (20)	1957
142	L'bro Cottages, L'bro Road (37)	1957
143	Vine Street (4)	1957
144	Pingle Street (6)	1957
145	Fuller Street (16)	1957
146	Mowbray Street (57)	1957
147	Jarrom Street (66)	1957
148	Basil Terrace, Basil Street (3)	1957
149	Albert Street (79)	1957

150–51	Middle Street and Mill Lane (228)	1957
152–54	Brudenell and Gray Streets (18)	1957
155	Abbey Gate (6)	1957
156	Martin Street and School Cottages (10) 1957	
157	Leadenhall Street (61)	1957
158–61	All Saints Road (161)	1958
162–66	Bath and Friday Streets (32)	1958
167–68	Great and Little Hole Streets etc (31)	1958
169–70	Coventry Street etc (46)	1958
171–72	Sanvey Lane Nos 1 and 2 (8)	1958
173–74	West Bridge Street etc (23)	1958
175–79	Richard Street etc (243)	1958
180–83	Hampden Street etc (43)	1958
184	St George's Cottages, Colton Street (4) 1958	
185–87	The Conery and Mill Hill (14)	1958
188	St Bernard Street (6)	1958
189	Northgate Street (2)	1958
190–91	Noble and Clara Streets (13)	1959
192–94	Sherrard Road etc (30)	1959
195	Vulcan Cottages, Vulcan Road (13)	1958
196	Old Milton Street (8)	1958
197–98	Crown and Raglan Streets (68)	1959
199	Bow Street (9)	1958
200	Cramant Cottages, King Street (6)	1958
201	Regent Road (7)	1959
202–03	Ashwell and Wellington Streets (23)	1959
204–06	Carlton and Clinton Streets (32)	1959
207–16	Checketts Road etc (133)	1959
216–19	Humb Terrace, Bell Lane etc (62)	1959
220	Merridale Road (109)	1959
221–22	Oxford Street and Grange Lane (10)	1959
223–24	Conduit Street Nos 1 and 2 (10)	1959
225–28	Upper Conduit and Goscote Streets (161) 1959	
229	Upper George Street (7)	1959
330	Brunswick Street (12)	1959
231–32	Denmark and Curzon Streets (386)	1960
233	Wilton Street (50)	1959
234–35	Willow and Spinner Streets (351)	1960
236–37	Darker Street and Butt Close Lane (10) 1960	
238	Clarence Street (3)	1960
239–40	Wanlip and Willow Bridge Streets (312) 1960	
241–42	Junction Road and Melton Street (25) 1960	
243	Bedford Street (4)	1960
244–47	Stanley, Willow and Cobden Streets (141) 1961	
248	Blake Street (7)	1960
249	Steins Lane (9)	1960
250	Royal East Street (9)	1960
251–53	Arthur, Nichols and Burton Streets (89) 1961	
254	Laxton Street (104)	1961

255	Whimpstone Cottages Upper Conduit Street (4)	1961
256–58	Arnold Street, Bright Street (99)	1962
259	Curzon Street (2)	1962
260–62	Queen Street and St George Street (30) 1962	
263–66	Palmer Street (19)	1962
265–66	Thurcaston Road (43)	1962
267	Syston Street (230)	1962
268–69	Emerald and Littleton Streets (286)	1962
270–71	Grundon and Bradgate Streets (46)	1962
272	Jarrom Street (22)	1962
273	Main Street, Humberstone (8)	1962
274–75	Birstall Street (219)	1963
276	Old Church Street, Aylestone (20)	1963
277–78	Main Street, Humberstone (5)	1963
279	Carpenters Yard, Humberstone (5)	1963
280	Sutherland Cottage (3)	1963
281–83	Waring, Upper Kent and Beal Streets (457)	1965
284–96	Upper Conduit Street (394)	1964
297–99	Saffron Hill, New Parks Road, and St Minerva Cottages (32)	1964
300	Berkley Street (6)	1964
301–02	Rawson Street (18)	1965
303	Gerrard Street (3)	1964
304	Majorie Grove, Ross Walk (6)	1964
305	Lincoln Cottages (4)	1964
306	Nottingham Road (4)	1964
307–13	Conduit Street (84)	1965*
314–16	Havelock, Outram and Gateway Streets (300)	1965*
317	Alice Street (37)	1965
318–20	Havelock, Clarendon and New Bridge Streets (195)	1965
321	Sanvey Lane (5)	1965
322	Oak Street (6)	1965
323	High Street, Evington (7)	1965
324	Argyle Street No. 1 (343)	1965
325	Albany Cottages, Brandon Street (3) 1965*	
326	Queens Grove, Brandon Street (13)	1965*
327–28	Argyle and Catherine Streets (396)	1965*
329	Brookside Cottages, Bowmars Lane (10) 1966*	
330	Nelson Street (6)	1966*
331	Evington Footpath (6)	1966*
332	Holland Cottages, Sutherland Street (4) 1966*	
333–37	Harding and Johnson Streets, Pasture Lane (46)	1967*
335–36	Berkley Street Nos 1 and 2	1967*
338–40	Morton Road (276)	1967*
341–43	Newmarket, Gilliver Street (21)	1968*
347–51	Charnwood, Farnham, Flint Street and Humberstone Road (207)	1967*
352–60	Humberstone Road Nos 4 and 5	1968*

361	Newmarket Street No. 2	1968
362–73	Charnwood Street Nos 4-9	1968*
374	Parry Street No. 2	1968*
379–81	Crafton Street	1969*
382–84	Wharf Street	1969*
389	St James Terrace (19)	1970*
390–91	Newington and Lexham Street (81)	1970*
392–93	Laundry Lane and St Bernard Street (70) 1970*	
394–97	Duchess Street, Bath Street and Malt Office Lane (Belgrave) (62)	1970*
398–402	Justice Street, Evans Street and Checketts Road (238)	1970*
405	Great Holme Street (325)	1970*
406–08	Dane and Andrew Streets (18)	1970*
409–14	Hinckley Road Nos 1–6 (10)	1970*
415	Leamington Street (2)	1971*
416–17	Great Holme Street No. 2 (6)	1971*
418–19	Noble Street (248)	1971*
420	Tudor Road (1)	1971*
421	Clara Street	1971*
422–23	King Richard's Road (3)	1971*
424	Catesby Street (411)	1971*
425	Hinckley Road No. 7 (2)	1971*
426	Fitzroy Street (2)	1971*
427	Cardinal Street (97)	1971*
428	Maidstone Road (10)	1971*
429–30	Aylestone Road	1970
431–32	Elmdale Street (38)	1972*
433–36	Vann and Shirley Streets (156)	1972*
437	Loughborough Road (5)	1972*
438–40	Sussex and Kent Streets (54)	1974
441	Cecil Gardens (7)	1974
442	Garfield Cotts, Donnington Street (4)	1974
443	Garendon Street (2)	1973*
444	Cromwell Road (46)	1974
445	Clifton Road (13)	1974
446–48	Saffron Lane and Cavendish Road (34) 1974	
449	Halstead Street (2)	1974
450–55	Ash, Oak and Larch Streets, Unity Avenue and Humberstone Road (210)	1974
456–85	Walnut Street (380)	1974
461	Earl Russel Street (4)	1974
464–69	Stoughton and Oxenden Streets (98) 1974*	
471	Butt Close (6)	1974*
472–78	Leire Street and Harrison Road (48)	1974*
479–84	Stonebridge and London Streets (44)	1975
485–87	Catherine, Bardolph and Martin Streets (317)	1975
488	Vulcan Road No. 2 (5)	1975

Archives and Primary Sources
Annual Reports of the City Medical Officer of Health
Leicester City Council, Regeneration and Culture Department (Planning)
Leicester City Council, Register of Houses in Clearance Areas
Leicester City Museums, Dennis A. Calow and L.A. Upton collections (Newarke Houses)
Leicester Oral History Archive
Minutes of the Health Committee, Leicester City Council
Minutes of the Highways and Sewerage Committee, Leicester Town Council
Minutes of the Housing and Town Planning Committee, Leicester City Council
The Author's Collection
The Leicester Mercury
The Record Office for Leicestershire, Leicester and Rutland

Newspapers and Periodicals
Leicester Daily Post
Leicester Evening Post
The Illustrated Leicester Chronicle
The Leicester Guardian
The Leicester Mercury
The Leicester Pioneer
The South Midlands Free Press
The Wyvern

Books and Pamphlets
Allen, F.W. *The Collection, Disposal, and Utilisation of Town Refuse in Leicester*, 1904.
Barclay, Tom *Memoirs and Medleys, The Autobiography of a Bottle Washer*, 1934.
Beazley, Ben *Postwar Leicester*, 2006.
Brown, Cynthia *Wharf Street Revisited: A History of the Wharf Street Area of Leicester*, 1995.
Burnett, J. *A Social History of Housing 1815–1971*, 1978.
Elliott, Malcolm *Victorian Leicester*, Leicester 1979.
Elliott, Malcolm *John Buck: Pioneer of Preventive Medicine and the Care of the Mentally Ill*, Transactions of the Leicestershire Archeological and Historical Society, Volume 64, 1990.
Gardiner, William *Music and Friends* Volume I, 1838.
Haynes, Barry *Working-Class Life in Victorian Leicester: The Joseph Dare Reports*, 1991.
Howes, C. (ed.) *Leicester: Its Civic, Industrial, Institutional and Social Life*, Leicester 1927.
Lancaster, Bill *Radicalism Cooperation and Socialism: Leicester Working Class Politics 1860–1906*, Leicester 1987.
Leicester City Council *Renewal Strategies, First Report*, May 1975.
Leicester Shelter Group *Bartholomew Street*, March 1975.
Leicestershire Multicultural Archive *Highfields Remembered*, 1996.
McKinley, R.A. (ed.) *Victoria County History, A History of the County of Leicester: volume 4: The City of Leicester*, 1958.
Millard, C. Killick MD *An Unsavoury but Important Feature of the Slum Problem*, 1932.
Muthesius, S. *The English Terraced House*, 1982.
Newitt, Ned *From Slums to Semis, Housing the People of Leicester, 1914–39*, MPhil Thesis, University of Leicester, 1992.
Ranger, William *Report to the General Board of Health on a Preliminary Inquiry into the Sewerage, Drainage, Supply of Water and Sanitary Condition of the Inhabitants of the Town of Leicester*, 1849.
Simmons, Jack *Leicester, Past and Present Volume 2*, 1974.
Simmons, Jack *A Victorian Social Worker: Joseph Dare and the Leicester Domestic Mission*, Transactions of the Leicestershire Archeological and Historical Society, Volume 46, 1970–71.
Simon, E.D. *The Anti-Slum Campaign*, 1933.
Underwood, John *The History of Sewerage and Sewage Treatment at Leicester*, 1886.
Waddington, R.G. *Leicester, the Making of a Modern City*, Leicester c.1930.

Printed by Printforce, United Kingdom